MW01414717

Win-Win Discipline

Strategies for All Discipline Problems

Dr. Spencer Kagan

Kagan

Kagan

© 2020 by ***Kagan Publishing***

This book is published by ***Kagan Publishing***. All rights are reserved by ***Kagan Publishing***. No part of this publication may be reproduced or transmitted in any form by any means, electronic or mechanical, including photocopy, recording, or any information storage and retrieval system, without prior written permission from ***Kagan Publishing***. The blackline masters included in this book are intended for duplication only by classroom teachers who purchase the book, for use limited to their own classrooms. To obtain additional copies of this book or information regarding professional development contact:

Kagan Publishing
981 Calle Amanecer
San Clemente, CA 92673
800.933.2667
www.KaganOnline.com

ISBN: 978-1-933445-66-3

Table of Contents

Introduction and Appreciations 4

Part I. The Building Blocks of Win-Win Discipline 7
    Chapter 1: The Building Blocks of Win-Win Discipline. . . . 9

Part II. Preventive Procedures 15
    Chapter 2: The Four Types of Disruptions: ABCD 17
    Chapter 3: Preventing ABCD Disruptions 25
    Chapter 4: The Seven Positions 31
    Chapter 5: Preventing Position-Based Disruptions 43

Part III. Responding in the Moment-of-Disruption 51
    Chapter 6: The ABCD Questions 53
    Chapter 7: Identifying Positions 67
    Chapter 8: Validating Positions 75
    Chapter 9: Responding to the Seven Positions. 83
    Chapter 10: Selected Moment-of-Disruption
                    Structures 95

Part IV. Follow-Ups 111
    Chapter 11: Following Up 113
    Chapter 12: Selected Follow-Up Structures 121

Part V. Conclusion 135
    Chapter 13: Conclusion 136

Part VI. Notes 137

About the Author 143
Resources 144

Introduction

Win-Win Discipline is based on very simple ideas:

1. **Disruptive behavior is an attempt to meet a need.**
2. **We can infer the need motivating disruptive behavior.**
3. **We can teach students responsible, nondisruptive ways to meet their needs.**
4. **When students learn to meet their needs in responsible ways, they win important life skills, and the teacher and classmates win a nondisruptive class. It is a Win-Win.**

As simple as these ideas are, Win-Win Discipline is a comprehensive approach to discipline. Win-Win includes ***Preventive Procedures,*** which structure the classrooms in ways student needs are met so they don't need to be disruptive. Win-Win also includes ***Strategies for the Moment-of-Disruption*** that end disruptions and guide students toward responsible behaviors, as well as Win-Win ***Follow-Ups***, what to do following disruptive behavior to reinforce responsible behavior and prevent future disruptions.

Traditionally, classroom discipline has been linked to punishment. The idea: punish disruptive behavior to make it less likely going forward. We have only to look at the incidences of disruptive behavior in schools where punishment is high to realize that approach is bankrupt. Punishment begets retaliation. Win-Win Discipline redefines discipline. Discipline is not something we do to students; it is something we help them acquire. Through Win-Win Discipline, students learn responsible ways to meet their needs so the need for disruptive behavior disappears. Win-Win Discipline is the opposite of punishment; it is caring for the disruptive student, teaching the disruptive student responsible ways to meet his or her needs.

Introduction

How This Book Is Organized

Part I. The Building Blocks of Win-Win Discipline. In Part I we introduce the building blocks of Win-Win Discipline. We identify (1) the four types of disruptive behavior, ABCD; (2) the seven positions from which disruptive behavior spring; and (3) the three pillars that define the philosophy of Win-Win Discipline. The pillars define our relationship with students and the goal of Win-Win Discipline: We adopt a same-side orientation toward our students and seek collaborative solutions in order to help students learn autonomous responsible behaviors that allow them to meet their needs without engaging in nonadaptive, disruptive behaviors.

Part II. Preventive Procedures. We use our knowledge of the four types of disruptive behaviors and the seven student positions to put in place an enormous number of preventive procedures. With the Win-Win preventive procedures in place, most disruptive behaviors never occur.

Part III. Responding in the Moment-of-Disruption. When a disruption does occur, we respond differentially depending on the type of behavior and the position of the student. Win-Win is the opposite of a one-size-fits-all approach. We respond to a student seeking attention in a very different way than to a student who is angry or seeking control. Our knowledge of the four types of behaviors and the seven positions allows us to tailor our response using preestablished Win-Win Discipline Moment-of-Disruption Structures.

Part IV. Follow-Ups. Some disruptive behaviors need no follow-up. But if a student is not progressing toward autonomous responsibility, we use preestablished Win-Win Discipline Follow-Up Structures to help students on the path toward responsibility.

Introduction

Part V. Conclusion. In the brief conclusion, we describe how Win-Win Discipline gives us a new set of lenses to view our students, empowering us to define discipline as something students acquire rather than something we do to students. Win-Win Discipline affirms our true role: We are educators; not disciplinarians.

Part VI. Notes. The last section is for note-taking. By recording what works, we become more reflective and shape our relationship with our students in ways that are a win for disruptive students, their classmates, and ourselves. Win-Win Discipline is liberating: We are freer to teach, and our students are freer to learn.

Appreciations

I am grateful for the support and professional input of Tom Finegan, the lead Win-Win Discipline Kagan Trainer. Tom had many suggestions to align the book with current discipline issues in schools to improve content. Miguel Kagan gave it strong editing and structural suggestions. Heather Malk designed the book, giving it a fresh look and readable style. Tony Swagler contributed his talented illustrations; Celso Rodriguez designed the Win-Win logo on the cover and the ABCD icons that give voice to letters; Kirsten Zanze proofread several passes; Becky Herrington oversaw the book design and production and liaisoned with all contributors; and Ginny Harvey copyedited the final version of the book. Throughout the process, this team provided me with formative input and support. I am very grateful to be part of a team of inspired educators and to have the support of a dedicated publishing team. I am grateful also for all the teachers who shared their stories of how Win-Win Discipline has transformed their classrooms and their relations with students. They have touched my heart.

—*Spencer Kagan*

Part I

The Building Blocks of Win-Win Discipline

Win-Win Discipline is built on four types of building blocks:

1. Understanding the four types of disruptive behavior. (ABCD Disruptions)
2. Distinguishing seven student positions that cause disruptive behavior. (7 Positions)
3. Mastering structures and strategies to prevent disruptions, respond effectively in the moment-of-disruption, and, when necessary, to follow up after a disruption. (Structures and Strategies: Follow-Ups, Moment-of-Disruption, Prevention)
4. Defining the goal of discipline as: Having students learn responsible, nondisruptive ways to meet their needs. Reaching that goal by adopting a "same-side" orientation toward students. And working with students to reach collaborative, win-win solutions. (The Three Pillars: Same-Side, Collaborative Solutions, Learned Responsibility)

Part I: The Building Blocks of Win-Win Discipline

In This Part

Chapter 1: The Building Blocks of Win-Win Discipline......9

The building blocks of Win-Win Discipline are symbolized as follows:

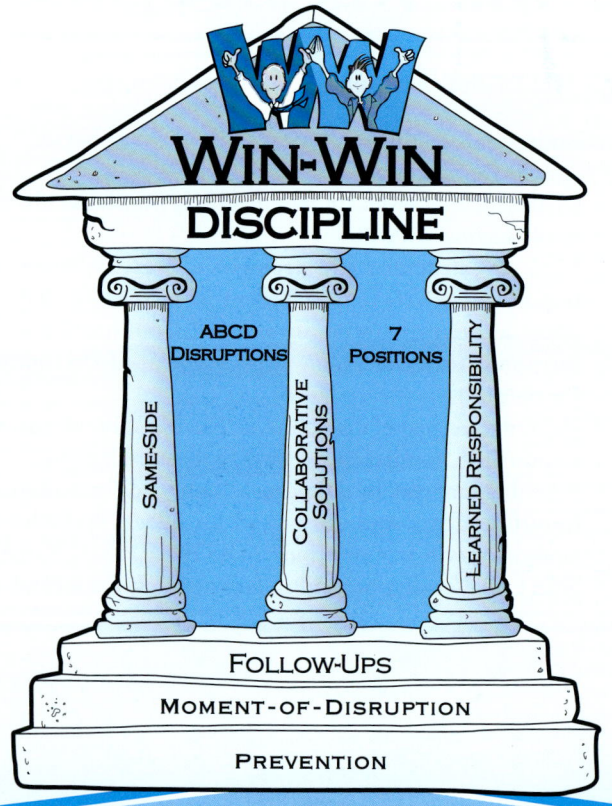

Win-Win Discipline

- ABCD Disruptions
- 7 Positions
- Same-Side
- Collaborative Solutions
- Learned Responsibility
- Follow-Ups
- Moment-of-Disruption
- Prevention

Chapter 1

The Building Blocks of Win-Win Discipline

Chapter 1: The Building Blocks of Win-Win Discipline

The ability to implement Win-Win Discipline is based on an understanding of four types of building blocks:

The Three Pillars

The three pillars symbolize the philosophy of Win-Win Discipline. They focus us on the ultimate goal, *Learned Responsibility,* and the two ways we reach that goal: by assuming a *Same-Side Orientation* with our students and by working with them to create *Collaborative Solutions.*

Same-Side

The teacher feels and communicates to the disruptive student that the teacher is on the same-side with the student, wants to team up with the student, identifies with the student, and understands where the student is coming from.

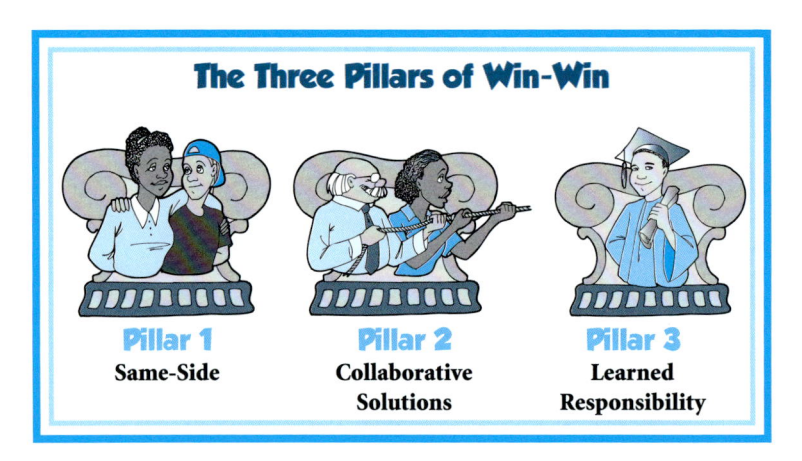

The Three Pillars of Win-Win

Pillar 1
Same-Side

Pillar 2
Collaborative Solutions

Pillar 3
Learned Responsibility

The Building Blocks of Win-Win Discipline

Collaborative Solutions
The student and teacher share the responsibility of cocreating discipline solutions. The discipline solution is not imposed on the student. It is something the student helps create.

Learned Responsibility
The Win-Win Discipline solution leads to critical new learning for the student. The student learns more responsible behaviors to meet his or her needs, so disruptions are less likely in the future. This third pillar, Learned Responsibility, is the ultimate goal of Win-Win Discipline. Win-Win aims not at merely ending disruptions; it aims at teaching positive, responsible behaviors. Win-Win is a positive educational program.

Although the three pillars of Win-Win are simple, they are powerful and transformative. The three pillars allow us to view our students and ourselves through a new set of lenses. Through the lenses of Win-Win, discipline methods that previously appeared adequate appear inadequate. For example, discipline strategies and approaches that aim at ending disruptions, even when they work, are viewed as inadequate if they do not result in students learning more responsible behavior.

Chapter 1: The Building Blocks of Win-Win Discipline

Learned responsibility is a process. As teachers, we use Win-Win structures and strategies to help students move from a disruptive orientation to a responsible orientation, as illustrated in the table: The Learned Responsibility Process.

The benefits of making Learned Responsibility the ultimate goal of a discipline program include:

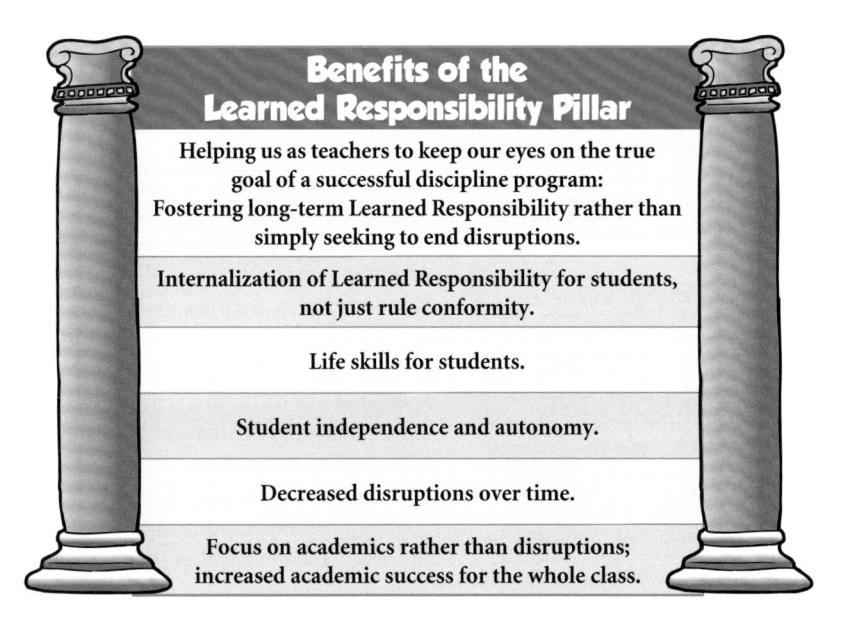

Benefits of the Learned Responsibility Pillar

Helping us as teachers to keep our eyes on the true goal of a successful discipline program: Fostering long-term Learned Responsibility rather than simply seeking to end disruptions.

Internalization of Learned Responsibility for students, not just rule conformity.

Life skills for students.

Student independence and autonomy.

Decreased disruptions over time.

Focus on academics rather than disruptions; increased academic success for the whole class.

The Building Blocks of Win-Win Discipline

The Learned Responsibility Process

Disruptive Orientation *Student Attempts to Fulfill Needs through Disruptive Behaviors*	Teacher-Mediation *Student Needs Fulfilled through Teacher-Initiated Procedures and Structures*	Responsible Orientation *Student Needs Fulfilled through Autonomous Responsible Behaviors*
Attention-Seeking	Teacher provides attention and helps student gain attention through responsible behaviors.	**Self-Validation**
Avoiding Failure	Teacher structures tasks for success and helps student transform "I can't" messages into "I can."	**Self-Confidence**
Angry	Teacher helps student deal with angry feelings in responsible ways.	**Self-Control**
Control-Seeking	Teacher provides choices and helps students internalize a sense of choice.	**Self-Determination**
Energetic	Teacher helps student channel energy into learning tasks.	**Self-Directing**
Bored	Teacher provides engaging, developmentally appropriate curriculum and instruction linked to student interest.	**Self-Motivated**
Socially Uninformed	Teacher informs student of appropriate behaviors.	**Self-Informing**

Win-Win Discipline
Kagan Publishing • 800.933.2667 • www.KaganOnline.com

ABCD Disruptions

Almost all disruptions are of one of four types, A, B, C, or D. That is, they are either ***Aggression, Breaking the Rules, Confrontation,*** or ***Disengagement.*** To create Win-Win solutions, we tailor our response to the type of disruption For example, we treat our response to aggressive behavior differently than we do for disengagement.

The Seven Positions

Almost all disruptive behavior springs from the need within the student. For examples, a student acting as a clown may be needing attention; a student refusing to do an assignment may be needing to assert control. The ability to recognize and respond appropriately to the position of a student determines the success of our discipline response. Win-Win Discipline is not a one-size-fits-all program because students are in different positions. The seven student positions are ***(1) Attention-Seeking; (2) Avoiding Failure; (3) Angry; (4) Control-Seeking; (5) Energetic; (6) Bored;*** and ***(7) Socially Uninformed.***

Three Types of Win-Win Strategies and Structures

A great deal of disruptive behavior never occurs if we deploy ***Win-Win Preventive Procedures.*** If a disruption does occur, we need ***Moment-of-Disruption Structures.*** Finally, when the teacher and students have cooled down following a disruption, we use ***Win-Win Follow-Ups*** to reinforce responsible behavior and prevent future disruptions.

Part II

Preventive Procedures

In Part II, we examine ways to prevent disruptive behaviors. Creating a classroom in which disruptive behavior does not occur is every teacher's dream. The dream is possible when we understand and implement preventive procedures for the four types of disruptive behaviors and structure so the needs of the seven positions are met before students attempt to satisfy those needs via disruptive behaviors.

In this part of the book, we first examine how to identify the four types of disruptive behaviors and how to prevent each. Then we examine the seven student positions and provide selected preventive procedures designed to meet the needs of each position.

Part II: Preventive Procedures

In This Part

Chapter 2: The Four Types of Disruptive Behavior: ABCD ...17

Chapter 3: Preventing ABCD Disruptions 25

Chapter 4: The Seven Positions 31

Chapter 5: Preventing Position-Based Disruptions..........43

Chapter 2

The Four Types of Disruptions: ABCD

Chapter 2: The Four Types of Disruptions: ABCD

Almost all disruptive behavior falls into one of four types: **A**ggression, **B**reaking the Rules, **C**onfrontation, and **D**isengagement—**ABCD**. We prevent each of these types of disruptions in different ways. For example, we prevent disengagement in very different ways than we prevent aggression.

Before examining how to prevent each type of disruption, let's identify each type.

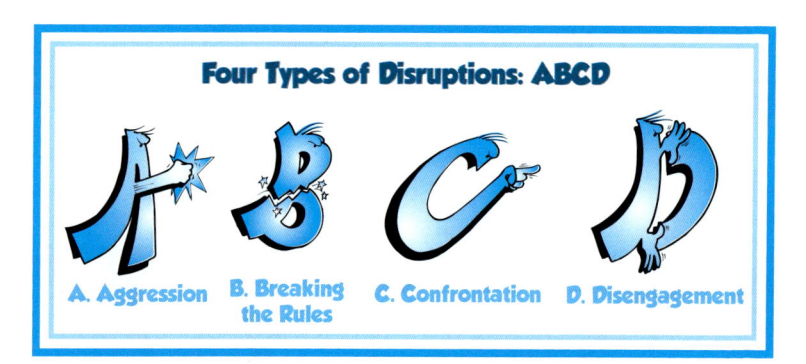

Four Types of Disruptions: ABCD

A. Aggression **B. Breaking the Rules** **C. Confrontation** **D. Disengagement**

The Four Types of Disruptions: ABCD

Aggression

Aggression comes in many forms. The essence of aggression is an attempt to hurt another. The aggressive act can aim to harm the other physically (hitting, biting, punching) or psychologically (put-downs, intimidation). It can take the form of verbal abuse (yelling, swearing) or gestures (giving "the finger," disdainful looks). It can be direct (hurting the person) or indirect (breaking someone's possession, putting down their family or friends). It can take subtle forms as well, as in the passive-aggressive student who is an expert at frustrating others by not giving them what they want. Whatever form it takes, the essence of aggression is action aimed at harming others.

Examples of Aggressive Behaviors

Direct Physical	Indirect Physical	Direct Verbal	Signs & Gestures	Indirect
Hitting	Destroying things	Put-downs	Disrespectful hand/finger displays	Insulting family, friends
Kicking	Throwing things	Swearing at	Making faces	Tattling on
Slapping	Taking possessions	Calling names, teasing	Body language of disdain	Insinuating poor taste
Biting	Hiding others' possessions	Insulting dress or possessions	Rolling eyes	Ignoring

Win-Win Discipline
Kagan Publishing • 800.933.2667 • www.KaganOnline.com

Chapter 2: The Four Types of Disruptions: ABCD

Breaking the Rules

Teachers, schools, and districts have different rules. Most rules can be derived from two basic principles: (1) show respect for others, and (2) do not disrupt learning. Rules which flow from those principles include not interfering with the teacher's ability to teach and not interfering with other students' ability to learn. Some schools, however, have many specific rules governing student behavior.

Examples of Breaking the Rules

Timeliness	Materials	Dress	Behavior
Unexcused absences	Destroying class materials	Wrong length, type of clothes	Public display of affection
Being late	Not bringing materials to class	Wearing drug and alcohol logos	Running in hallways
Turning in assignments late	Writing in textbooks	Not wearing school uniform	Inappropriate Web sites
Not returning permission slips	Not following science lab rules	Wearing gang-related colors, insignias	Texting

The Four Types of Disruptions: ABCD

Confrontation

When we hear a "You can't make me," we know we are dealing with a confrontation. A confrontation is a power play. The student verbally or nonverbally asserts that the teacher is not in charge, shows disrespect for the teacher, or attempts to undermine the teacher's authority. There are many forms of confrontation including: aggression and disrespect toward the teacher, refusing to obey or do assignments, and instigating other class members toward disobedience or disrespect for the teacher.

Examples of Confrontational Behaviors

Aggression Toward Teacher	Disrespect	Refusing	Instigating
Hitting	Talking back	Refusing to do assignments	Repeated complaining
Profanity	Flirting with teacher, sexual innuendo	Refusing to sit, move, obey: "You can't make me"	Taking charge, telling others what to do
Arguing with teachers	Contradicting, interrupting	Doing the opposite	Modeling disobedience
Putting down the teacher	Disdainful facial expressions toward teacher	Refusing to participate	Initiating rebellion; putting down the task

Win-Win Discipline
Kagan Publishing • 800.933.2667 • www.KaganOnline.com

Chapter 2: The Four Types of Disruptions: ABCD

Disengagement

The fourth type of disruptive behavior is disengagement. The other three types of disruptive behaviors usually disrupt the teacher and/or the rest of the class. Disengagement can be a solo disruption, involving only the disengaged student. It is tempting to ignore the student who is disengaged, as the student may not be disrupting anyone else. But in Win-Win Discipline, we define a discipline problem as anything that disrupts the teaching/learning process, even if only one student is disrupted. We take disengagement seriously—it goes to the heart of what we define as a discipline problem. Disengagement can take many forms, including off-task behaviors, tuning out, or random activity.

Examples of Disengagement

Off Task – Behavior	Off Task – Verbal	Tuning Out	Hyperactivity
Watching YouTube videos	Asking off-subject questions	Sleeping	Horseplay
Wandering	Blurting out	Daydreaming	Carelessly rushing through work
Performing wrong task	Playing dumb	Head on desk	Laughing, giggling
Grooming	Socializing	Doodling	Fidgeting with materials

The Four Types of Disruptions: ABCD

Classifying Disruptive Behaviors

By classifying disruptive behaviors into only four types, we make discipline more manageable. Knowing which type of disruptive behavior is most common in our classroom or by a specific individual, we can respond more appropriately.

Classifying Disruptions: Two Rules
It is very helpful to use two rules when classifying disruptive behavior using the ABCD category system:

Rule 1. Three Before B
Rule 2. Teacher-Directed Aggression = Confrontation

Rule 1: Three Before B
Use the Breaking the Rules category only if the behavior does not fit any of the other three categories.

ABCD categories are not mutually exclusive. When a student hits another student, the student is breaking a rule and is being aggressive. When a student goes to sleep during class, the student is breaking a rule and is disengaged. How then do we classify the behavior? Follow this rule: **Three Before B.**

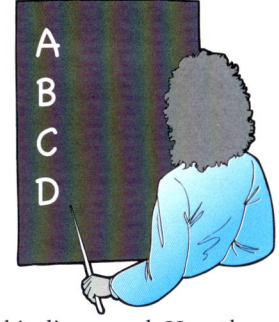

The reason we try first to classify the behavior as Aggression, Confrontation, or Disengagement is that those categories are more specific. Breaking the Rules covers many things, so it gives us the least amount of information. Knowing a student is Aggressive gives us much more information about how to respond in the moment-of-disruption than does knowing the student is Breaking a Rule.

Chapter 2
The Four Types of Disruptions: ABCD

Rule 2: Aggression Toward the Teacher = Confrontation
Aggression toward the teacher is not classified as Aggression, but rather as Confrontation.

A teacher says, "Your assignment tonight is to solve the problems on pages 10 through 12." A student calls out, "You B----!"

Swearing at someone is aggression, but refusing to accept an assignment from the teacher is also a confrontation. How shall we classify this disruption? The rule is: **Classify aggression toward the teacher as Confrontation.**

Aggression toward the teacher is usually a form of protest. We have very different strategies for preventing and dealing with Confrontation than we do for preventing and dealing with Aggression. When there is aggression toward the teacher, more often than not we will be more successful responding to the confrontation than the aggression (unless of course there is a threat to someone's safety). Why? Learning to control one's aggression does not deal with the problem. It controls only the symptom. If the student is in conflict with the teacher, the most fundamental issue is dealing with the confrontation. If we are successful in that, the aggression disappears.

Chapter 3

Preventing ABCD Disruptions

Chapter 3

Preventing ABCD Disruptions

The first step in preventing ABCD disruptions is to determine which types of disruptions are occurring most frequently in the class and by individual students who are frequently disruptive. For this, we use the ABCD Tally that directs us toward appropriate preventive procedures.

The ABCD Tally

Using the two rules for categorizing ABCD disruptions, the teacher tallies the frequency of disruptions for the class and for individual students who have been disruptive frequently. The ABCD Tally is very helpful in directing the teacher to the appropriate preventive procedures for frequent disruptions within a class and for frequent disruptions by an individual.

A. Preventing Aggression

The Individual ABCD Tally directs the teacher toward appropriate preventive procedures for individuals who have been disruptive frequently. See the sample Individual ABCD Tally form below.

Sample Individual ABCD Tally

	Monday	Tuesday	Wednesday	Thursday	Friday	Total
Aggression	|||						5
Breaking the Rules								2
Confrontation							1
Disengagement							1

Use the Individual ABCD Tally to identify the type of disruptive behaviors displayed by an *individual student.*

Preventing ABCD Disruptions

Given an Individual ABCD Tally that looks like the one on previous page, a Win-Win teacher would establish with the student preventive procedures that make aggression less likely. The book, *Win-Win Discipline*, provides numerous ways to prevent aggressive behavior including establishing cool-down procedures, teacher nonverbal signals to students whose emotions are escalating, cool-down areas, conflict resolution training, peer mediators, and learning how to disagree agreeably. Implementing cooperative learning teambuilding and classbuilding activities dramatically reduces the incidence of disruptive behaviors.

B. Preventing Rule Infractions

Sample Class ABCD Tally

	Monday	Tuesday	Wednesday	Thursday	Friday	Total
Aggression	||	||	|||	|	||	10
Breaking the Rules	||||||	|||||	||||||	||||	||||	25
Confrontation	||	|		|	|	5
Disengagement	|		||	|	|	5

Use the Class ABCD Tally to record and classify all *class* disruptions.

Given a Class ABCD Tally that looks like the one above, a Win-Win teacher would determine if students recall the rules, understand the rules, and have the ability and willingness to apply the rules. The book, *Win-Win Discipline*, provides numerous ways to ensure rules are understood, remembered, and applied. Guidelines are provided

Chapter 3

Preventing ABCD Disruptions

for having the class generate class rules, creating rules posters, rules T-charts, and rules reminders. Emphasis is placed on activities to foster understanding and identifying with the purpose of each rule.

C. Preventing Confrontations

Students will sometimes confront a teacher, refusing to do what the teacher has requested. Many confrontations are a form of aggression—aggression directed at the teacher. Some can be a very calm refusal to go along with whatever the teacher has proposed for the class or the student.

Like aggression, confrontations occur for many reasons. Most often a confrontation is a power play in which a student is asserting control: "You can't tell me what to do, I'm in charge of me." The need to feel in charge of oneself is positive. But students trying to establish a sense of control may do so in inappropriate ways or at inappropriate times.

To prevent confrontations, Win-Win Discipline side-steps power plays with students and instead adopts a "We" approach. Among the many preventive procedures detailed in the *Win-Win Discipline* book are: involving students in the generation of class norms and rules, allowing students to make many decisions and choices, including a student suggestion box, structuring class meetings, and using phrases that deflate confrontation. For example, when a student says an assignment is stupid, we use the "To you…To me…" gambit: "To you it may seem stupid; to me it is very important because…"

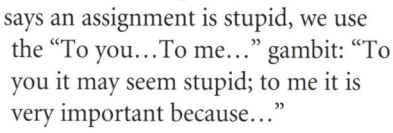

Preventing ABCD Disruptions

D. Preventing Disengagement

Students become disengaged when:

- **The learning task is too difficult or too easy (not developmentally appropriate)**
- **Instructional strategies are repetitive and isolating (boring worksheet work)**
- **Work is meaningless, lacks relevance to the student**
- **Management procedures create long wait times**

For example, if a teacher passes out papers one at a time, it leaves plenty of time for students to become disengaged. If instead, the teacher says, "Materials Monitors in each team, quickly and quietly come up and get supplies for your teams," the papers are distributed quickly and there is little time for disengagement.

To prevent disengagement, the Win-Win teacher focuses on what we call the Big 3: Curriculum, Instruction, and Management. When the curriculum is engaging, delivered in an engaging way, with crisp management techniques, students seldom become disengaged.

The *Win-Win Discipline* book describes in detail many procedures to prevent disengagement. To list a few:

Engaging Curriculum

- **Making curriculum relevant and developmentally appropriate**
- **Creating engaging learning centers**
- **Including progressive sponges**

Win-Win Discipline
Kagan Publishing • 800.933.2667 • www.KaganOnline.com

Chapter 3: Preventing ABCD Disruptions

Engaging Instruction
- Employing a variety of instructional strategies
- Using dynamic visuals
- Engaging the multiple intelligences

Engaging Management
- Starting the class with Ready, Set, Go work
- Adopting hand signals
- Triggering instructions
- Using simultaneous management techniques

Chapter 4

The Seven Positions

Chapter 6

The Seven Positions

Whereas student disruptive behaviors are what a student does, student positions are the place the student is in that leads to the disruptive behavior. For example, a student seeking attention may act like a clown or make funny noises to attract attention. We never accept disruptive behaviors, but paradoxically, by accepting and even validating student positions, we radically reduce the need for disruptive behaviors. See the table below: Disruptive Behaviors vs. Positions.

Disruptive Behaviors vs. Positions

	Disruptive Behaviors	Positions
What is it?	What Students Do	Why They Do It
Where does it come from?	Attempt to Meet Needs	Rooted in Human Condition
How do we recognize it?	Observable	Inferred
Win-Win Philosophy	Disruption Not Accepted	Position Validated

The Seven Positions

Almost all disruptive behavior springs from one or more student positions. The positions are illustrated as follows:

The Seven Positions

1. Attention-Seeking
2. Avoiding Failure
3. Angry
4. Control-Seeking
5. Energetic
6. Bored
7. Socially Uninformed

A Note About the Win-Win Characters: The Win-Win Discipline students illustrated here are intentionally from different cultures and genders to underscore the notion that all genders and ethnicities experience all seven positions. In no way does an illustration of a particular gender or ethnicity suggest that any specific group of students is more likely to come from one of the seven positions. These seven positions are part of the human condition and most of us experience most, if not all, of these positions at different times.

Win-Win Discipline
Kagan Publishing • 800.933.2667 • www.KaganOnline.com

The Seven Positions

1. Attention-Seeking

We all need attention. It is rooted in our biology. Infants who did not cry when too long abandoned had a lower probability of survival. Humans, given their initial extreme dependency (a horse walks at birth; humans take a year), need the attention of others, especially adult others.

Attention-seeking is a universal need, and we all have many ways of seeking positive attention. Some students, however, at times attempt to fill their need for attention in inappropriate ways, such as clowning around, talking back, or shouting out answers. The need for attention can be so strong at times that students will even strive for negative attention as in the case of the student who bragged, "The teacher screamed louder at me than at you." Inappropriate ways of seeking attention, of course, can be very disruptive. If we satisfy the need for attention among students on a regular basis, they have less need to act disruptively.

2. Avoiding Failure

No one likes to fail. And we strive especially hard not to fail if the failure will result in public embarrassment. Students will become disruptive if it is the only way to avoid failure, especially a failure that will lead to public embarrassment or a negative internal attribution. A student may refuse to do an assignment if it is less painful to say to himself and others, "I just didn't feel like doing it," than to risk the possibility of failure.

The Seven Positions

How we structure our classrooms will determine to a large extent how many students need to be disruptive to avoid failure. Contrast two scenarios:

Classroom A: "Your homework is the problems on pages 10 to 11. Tomorrow we will grade your homework by trading papers with someone in the class. The grades will be posted this week. You should find these problems easy. If you do miss any of the problems, you will be assigned to a tutoring group, depending on the type of problem you miss the most."

Classroom B: "Your homework is the problems on pages 10 to 11. Tomorrow you will be able to grade your own homework in class. No one will be allowed to see anyone else's homework; you are not to share grades. After we grade the homework, all students will choose one tutoring group to join, depending on the type of problem they would like to work on."

The student who fears public embarrassment associated with failure is much more likely to do the homework assignment in Classroom B than in Classroom A because the chance for public embarrassment is reduced.

3. Angry

Anger is a natural reaction in many situations, including but not limited to:

- Aggression
- Defeat
- Fear
- Frustration
- Humiliation
- Inhibiting impulses
- Jealousy
- Loss
- Moral outrage
- Pain
- Threat

The Seven Positions

An angry outburst can be the result of several of these situations in combination, like the straw that broke the camel's back. For example, students coming in after losing at a sporting activity on the playground are much more predisposed toward an angry outburst in the face of a frustrating learning experience than those who won on the playground. Students may not be aware of what has predisposed them toward a display of anger; when asked why they got angry, they probably would not mention the playground defeat even if it were a factor.

Many factors can create anger. Frustration—trying hard repeatedly and not succeeding at the task—eventually makes most of us want to break whatever we are working on. Feeling that we have been treated unfairly, whether or not the treatment was actually unfair, leads to a sense of moral outrage that can trigger an angry outburst. The attribution process plays an important role in anger as well. Interesting experiments show that a person being treated rudely is far less likely to feel angry toward the tormentor if he or she finds out that this individual has been suffering in his or her personal life. Generalizing from this experiment, we might predict that students will display less anger toward each other if the norm is to share about personal upsets, and that a teacher might do well to model sharing when things are not going well, rather than putting on a face.

Anger is part of life, including life in a classroom. Classrooms are about learning, and learning new material is often associated with frustration, inhibition of impulses, persistence in the face of difficulties, threat to one's ego, and jealousy of those for whom the learning comes more easily. Thus, the potential for anger is always present, so as teachers we need to look at many ways we can lower that potential, as well as putting in smooth, practiced procedures for occasions when angry outbursts occur.

4. Control-Seeking

None of us wants to feel like a pawn, moved about by forces beyond our control. Who wants to be told what to do, how to do it, and when to have it done? We relish the experience of personal choice; we want to feel in charge of ourselves. The experience of choosing, while difficult for some and at times fraught with anxiety, gives us our sense of freedom. We all strive to seek control of our lives in various ways.

A great deal of research on learned helplessness shows that all organisms become depressed when they can't control their outcomes.[1] In extreme cases, when we can't control our outcomes, "feel good" neurotransmitters become depleted and the result is clinical depression. The need to feel a sense of control is rooted in our biology.

The need for control can take many forms. The student who asks if he or she can do an essay rather than take a test is attempting to take control. The student in a cooperative learning team who tells everyone else what to do is attempting to take control. The student who refuses to do an assignment may be trying to prove, "No one tells me what to do." Obviously, control seeking can lead to disruptive behaviors.

By recognizing and validating students' need for control by, for example, allowing students many choices, we prevent disruptions because students do not have to be disruptive to fill their need for control.

5. Energetic

In an interesting experiment years ago, normal people were admitted to mental hospitals as patients as a test of how normal people act and are treated in abnormal environments. One of the things these pseudo-patients noted is that they found themselves pacing the halls. In the logbook of one of the patients, it was noted that the patient engaged in "abnormal pacing behavior."

When asked about this later, the man, who in his real life was an active person, simply explained that he was accustomed to exercise and that the only way he could get the exercise he needed in the mental hospital was to pace.

The need to move, to touch and manipulate things, is basic. Primary teachers spend a great deal of time socializing students to sit in one place. If the need to move is strong enough, it overrides that socialization. By including plenty of opportunities for movement, including work with hands-on manipulatives and class-building structures in which students get up from their seats and move in the room, teachers can prevent disruptive expressions of energy. When the need to move and express oneself physically is met on a regular basis, energetic students do not have to disrupt the class to fill their need.

6. Bored

Boredom is the opposite of peak experience. Mihaly Csikszentmihalyi, a Harvard psychologist, explains both boredom and peak experience in his classic book, *Flow*.[2] Flow occurs when there is an optimal relationship between student ability and task difficulty. All of us have experienced moments of flow—when we are totally engaged in an activity, time seems to disappear, we are tremendously productive, and there is a sense of effortlessness in our work. Csikszentmihalyi explains that this optimal experience occurs when the task we are working on matches our ability. If we work on a task that is too difficult for our ability level, we feel anxiety and have the impulse to stop the work. If we work on a task that is too easy for our ability, we feel boredom and lose interest. Everyone has the need to avoid boredom and avoid anxiety—we are happy when we are in a state of flow.

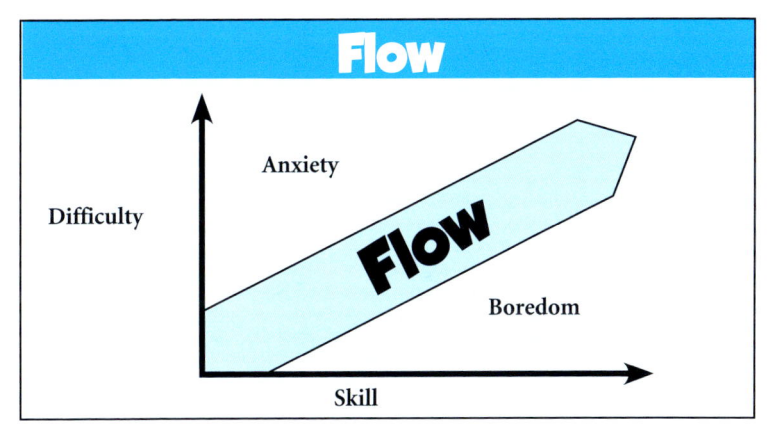

Flow

Difficulty (vertical axis), *Skill* (horizontal axis), *Anxiety* (above the flow band), *Boredom* (below the flow band), *Flow* (diagonal band)

A student who is not engaged in a learning task because it is too easy or because it is not of interest may seek stimulation in alternative ways—some of which can be disruptive to others. In the extreme case, a student punches another student not out of anger, but simply to "get something going." The student is seeking stimulation in a disruptive way. When we provide learning tasks that match student ability level, make the tasks intrinsically interesting, and provide the rationale for doing the tasks, we avoid boredom and reduce or eliminate the need for students to seek stimulation in disruptive ways.

Chapter 6

The Seven Positions

7. Socially Uninformed

Alex punches Pete in the shoulder. Alex is not angry, he is not bored, he is not seeking control, nor is he seeking attention. At home and in Alex's neighborhood, a punch in the shoulder is simply a way of relating. Alex does not know that the rules of appropriate behavior at school are different. He is uninformed about school social norms. Sandy uses a curse word. She hears profanity at home and in her neighborhood all the time and simply hasn't realized yet that the rules of appropriate behavior at school are different.

Being socially uninformed is not just being able to state the rules of the game. A teacher tells Alex there is no punching allowed in school and tells Sandy that profanity is forbidden. Alex still punches and Sandy still uses profanity. To paraphrase Mark Twain, "Tellin' ain't teachin'." After telling Alex and Sandy the social norms, they are still socially uninformed. It will take time for them to learn and consistently apply the rules of appropriate behaviors. We don't learn all the rules overnight, especially if we have spent a lifetime playing by different rules.

Brain research has distinguished different types of memory systems, located in different parts of the brain. It turns out that the way we remember what we ate for dinner last night (episodic memory), the way we remember the names of the ten amendments (semantic memory), and the way we remember how to drive a car (procedural memory) are very different, involving whole different brain systems. The way we remember "the rules of the game," which behaviors are right and wrong in which environments, is a type of procedural memory, and procedural memory is produced by repetition. Thus, for students to be informed, the Win-Win teacher must explain the rules many times in many ways and provide rehearsal and practice opportunities. Even if a student has been told the rules several times, the student may remain in the socially uninformed position. In Win-Win, we use the term "socially uninformed" to describe a student who has not yet obtained procedural memory of a responsible behavior. Becoming socially informed is a process, not a one-time event.

Positions Are Needs

Each of the seven student positions is associated with basic needs. If these needs are met on a regular basis within the classroom, students are unlikely to be disruptive. If, however, the only way a student can meet those needs is to be disruptive, disruptions will be frequent. Understanding the simple reality that disruptions are attempts to meet needs gives us great power in preventing them. All we have to do is recognize, understand, accept, and relate to these seven basic needs as we structure what goes on in our classroom.

Understanding the Positions

We can try to understand the seven positions objectively, seeing how the positions spring from the human condition and understanding their origin in evolution, biology, and brain structure and function. But there is another, even more important way to understand the seven positions—subjectively.

Unless we can identify with the positions, feel what it is like to be in each position, walk in the shoes of those in each position, know the position from the inside, we will never realize the highest potential of a Win-Win teacher. We will never be as sharp as possible at recognizing the positions or taking the "same-side" with disruptive students.

The position you most need to work on is the one you least recognize in yourself. It will be the position you will have the most difficulty with in your classroom. We tend to react negatively to traits in others that we will not readily accept in ourselves. Since we all have all the positions, if you find yourself reacting strongly to a disruptive behavior pattern in a student, try to determine which of the seven positions that student is exhibiting and work toward recognizing that same position in yourself.

References

[1] Seligman, M. *Helplessness: On Depression, Development, and Death.* San Francisco, CA: W.H. Freeman and Company, 1975.

[2] Csikszentmihalyi, M. *Flow: The Psychology of Optimal Experience.* New York, NY: HarperCollins Publishers, 1990.

Chapter 5

Preventing Position-Based Disruptions

Chapter 5

Preventing Position-Based Disruptions

Each disruption springs from the position of a student. The student who is angry may do something destructive, hit or insult a classmate, or simply pout and refuse to do an assignment. Different procedures prevent disruptions based on the seven positions.

Preventing Position-Based Disruptions

1. Attention-Seeking

The Win-Win teacher accepts that the need for attention is part of the human condition and provides students with ample positive attention, knowing attention fills a need and that if students receive positive attention on an ongoing basis, they will be far less likely to seek attention in disruptive ways.

Among the many ways we can provide students positive attention are to greet students at the door, express appreciation, acknowledge and validate student positions, use student names in examples, and spend time with each student individually. Using Kagan Cooperative Learning Structures provides students positive attention from their teammates and classmates. These and many other ways of providing positive attention are described in the book, *Win-Win Discipline.*

Preventing Position-Based Disruptions

2. Avoiding Failure

Whenever possible, the Win-Win teacher avoids putting students in situations which could result in public embarrassment.

Some strategies to avoid having classmates see a poor performance include giving private feedback, using cooperative learning structures that provide immediate coaching, guided practice and checking for understanding before having students work alone, and creating private signals so students can ask for help unobtrusively.

Among the many tools to prevent avoidance of failure described in the *Win-Win Discipline* book are teaching students gambits for asking for help, asking for clarification, and checking for understanding. For example, we teach students gambits to check for their understanding, like:

- *"Let me be sure I have this. Please watch me as I work this problem."*
- *"Let me put that in my own words to see if I understand."*
- *"Can you please give me a tip?"*

3. Angry

A great deal of research has been done about anger. It turns out that many of us grew up with a common misconception. We believed that it is always good to "get one's anger out." The belief in the benefits of catharsis or venting one's anger sprang from the psychoanalytic notion that repressed emotions had to become conscious

Chapter 5: Preventing Position-Based Disruptions

for rational decision making to prevail. It turns out, however, that venting one's anger often reignites the flames that need to die down before rational thought can take over. As teachers, it is usually best that we leave the catharsis and venting approaches to the psychologists and instead concentrate on preventing arousal of anger and helping students calm down once they have become angry.

We go a long way to prevent anger by preventing the major causes of anger among students: frustration, physical or psychological threats, pain, and a sense of being treated unfairly. Among the ways to prevent angry outbursts detailed in the book *Win-Win Discipline* are to monitor frustration levels, break up learning tasks, apply rules and positive attention equally, teach anger-control techniques, and teach students how to disagree politely with gambits like:

- *"I see it differently."*
- *"I would say that a little differently."*
- *"I have a different opinion about that."*
- *"Have you thought about this…?*

4. Control-Seeking

None of us wants to feel like a leaf in the wind, at the mercy of powers beyond our control. At certain ages, students go through a stage of separating themselves from adult authority and are especially concerned with developing autonomy. The impulse to establish independence is healthy. But if it

Preventing Position-Based Disruptions

takes the form of rejecting all adult authority or testing adult authority at every opportunity, it can be quite disruptive in the classroom. The best way to prevent disruptions rooted in the student's need for control is to sidestep any power plays and to give students as much autonomy, independence, choice, and control as is consistent with good instruction and good classroom management.

In the *Win-Win Discipline* book, we detail many ways to give students control, including giving students choices, giving students independent responsibilities, assigning students roles, validating student need for control, and having class meetings in which the class can make decisions. Use of Kagan Cooperative Learning decision-making structures like Spend-A-Buck and Sum-the-Ranks offers students the opportunity to make collaborative decisions.

5. Energetic

We all have energy and we all need to use it. The experience of being "antsy" after sitting through a long lecture is common to most of us. We are built to move. When the need to move is unsatisfied long enough, it interferes with clear thinking and learning. The Win-Win teacher recognizes and accepts the need for movement and incorporates movement into classroom activities in many ways.

Chapter 5: Preventing Position-Based Disruptions

Among the movement activities described in the *Win-Win Discipline* book are Silly Sports & Goofy Games, classbuilders, energizers, and student roles that involve movement, like Roving Reporter and Materials Monitor. Many Kagan Cooperative Learning Structures incorporate movement without time away from the curriculum, like Quiz-Quiz-Trade, StandUp–HandUp–PairUp, and Mix-Pair-Share.

6. Bored

As teachers, we must be careful to distinguish true boredom from feigned boredom. Pseudo-boredom may occur for a number of reasons, but the most common is an attempt to avoid the embarrassment associated with a public failure. Fearing failure, the student says, "Oh, I don't care about that." The student is feigning boredom to mask a fear of failure: It is much less embarrassing to say, "I don't care," than, "I'm afraid." We treat pseudo-boredom, which is really just disguised fear of failure, in the same way we treat any fear of failure—we make sure the student knows he or she can succeed.

We treat true boredom by generating motivation and interest. Motivating and interesting curriculum and instruction is nothing short of good teaching. Teachers who engage students do not experience disruptions based on boredom.

Among the ways we enhance student engagement is to make the curriculum relevant to student interests, relate curriculum to class and school, have students generate curriculum-related questions, use novel and surprising instructional strategies, and have students gather

Preventing Position-Based Disruptions

information from alternative sources such as interviews, magazines, documentaries, and student-designed experiments.

The *Win-Win Discipline* book includes descriptions of how to enhance engagement via projects, centers, multiple intelligences, choices, and matching task difficulty to student ability.

7. Socially Uninformed

On the first day of class, Johnny comes late to class, interrupts others, talks out of turn, and/or does not pick up after himself. It turns out that Johnny is not trying to be disruptive and actually would like to be a good student. He is simply acting the way kids in his home and neighborhood behave. He has not learned that there are different social norms for behavior at school. He is socially uninformed. The Win-Win response to a student who is socially uninformed is to find ways to help the student know and identify with school and classroom norms. It is not enough to know a rule; we work to make rule adherence part of procedural memory—it is just the way we do things in school. The goal: following school and class rules becomes as easy and automatic as riding a bike.

Chapter 5: Preventing Position-Based Disruptions

Among the Win-Win approaches to helping students who are socially uninformed are to assign a buddy to monitor for rule understanding and compliance, have students practice procedures, and establish verbal and nonverbal cues to prompt desired behavior. Multiple intelligences approaches can be used to help students know and remember the rules:

- **Verbal/Linguistic**
  Students write a poem about the rules.

- **Logical/Mathematical**
  Students derive reasons for the rules.

- **Visual/Spatial**
  Students make a poster to support the rules.

- **Musical/Rhythmic**
  Students write a rule rap, chant, or song.

- **Bodily/Kinesthetic**
  Students act out the rules.

- **Naturalist**
  Students create an analogy from nature.

- **Interpersonal**
  Students teach the rules to a partner.

- **Intrapersonal**
  Students keep a journal about the rules.

Part III

Responding in the Moment-of-Disruption

In this part of the book, we examine ways to respond in the moment of a disruption. By preparing our discipline responses prior to disruptions, we can better achieve Win-Win solutions. How we respond depends on the type of disruption, (A, B, C, or D), and the position of the student. By using well-established Win-Win moment-of-disruption structures that correspond to the type of disruption and the position of the student, we can efficiently end a disruption and foster learned responsibility.

In the emergency of a disruption, we can respond with well-practiced responses or respond based on our impulses. We are quite likely to later regret impulse-driven responses. If we trust our impulses, we are quite likely to model the very behavior we are trying to prevent.

Part III: Responding in the Moment-of-Disruption

In This Part

Chapter 6: The ABCD Questions 53

Chapter 7: Identifying Positions 67

Chapter 8: Validating Positions 75

Chapter 9: Responding to the Seven Positions..............83

Chapter 10: Selected Moment-of-Disruption Structures 95

Chapter 6

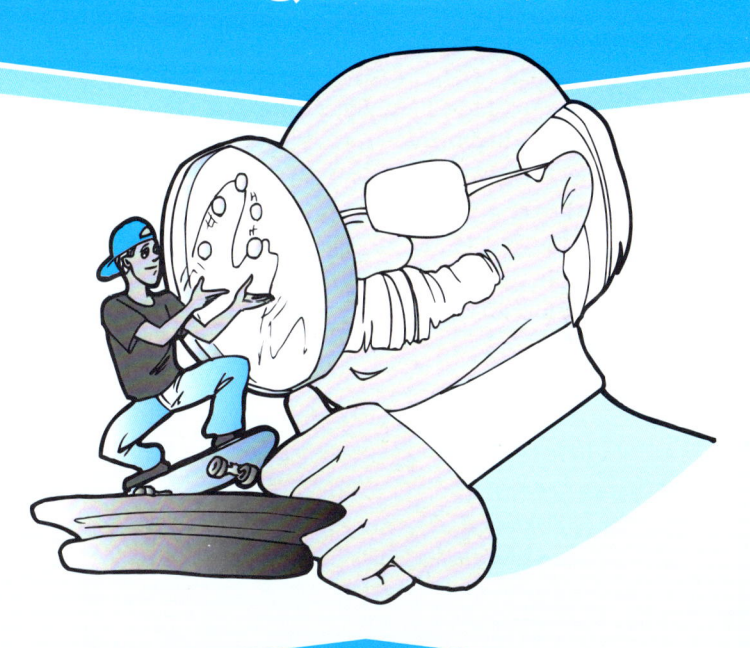

The ABCD Questions

Chapter 6: The ABCD Questions

One powerful tool in preparing Win-Win responses for the moment-of-disruption is to know and be ready to ask yourself critical disruption-specific questions for each of the ABCD behaviors. For example, if a student is acting aggressively, the first thing we need to know is whether the student is a threat to self or others. Our response will depend in part on that answer. For each of the ABCD disruptive behaviors, there are three critical questions we ask to help us formulate our response. The Disruption-Specific questions we need to ask:

Disruption-Specific ABCD Questions:

A. Aggression
1. Is there a **threat** to self or others?
2. Am I using **self-control**?
3. How can I teach **student self-control**?

B. Breaking the Rules
1. Does the student **know** the rule?
2. How can I promote **understanding** and **buy-in**?
3. Can the student reliably **apply** the rule?

C. Confrontation
1. Am I using **self-control**?
2. Can I provide the student with **choices**?
3. Am I using a Win-Win **leadership style**?

D. Disengagement
1. How can I **reengage** the student?
2. Is my **curriculum** engaging and relevant? Developmentally appropriate?
3. Is my **instruction** engaging? Am I using structures for engagement?
4. Is my **management** engaging? Am I decreasing time off task?

The ABCD Questions

The disruption-specific ABCD questions direct us to specific responses that promote Win-Win solutions and learned responsibility. Let's overview our responses.

A. Aggression

1. Is there a **threat to self or others?**

Aggressive behavior can be dangerous to others physically and psychologically. As teachers, our first concern is for the safety of everyone in our classroom. We need to prevent or terminate threatening or aggressive behavior quickly, not only because aggressive behavior is unsafe, but also because it can trigger more aggressive behavior via retaliation or contagion.

The *Win-Win Discipline* book includes a number of structures that are helpful if a student is a threat to self or others including:

- **Cool Down Reminder:** *"Are we getting close to needing cool down?"*
- **Cool Down:** *"Please take some time in the cool-down area now."*
- **Target, Stop, Do:** *"Susie, right now you are poking Sarah; the responsible thing to do is keep your hands to yourself and open your book to page 112."*

2. Am I using **self-control?**

In the heat of aggression, even when aggression is not directed toward the teacher, it is important for us to monitor our own reaction. Aggression begets aggression. If we are calm, we can defuse emotions and model a more rational approach.

Chapter 6: The ABCD Questions

The importance of remaining calm in the face of aggression is underscored by recent brain research revealing the existence of mirror neurons. When we read the faces of those around us, mirror neurons fire to produce the emotions in us that mirror the emotions projected by the faces around us. We are genetically wired to be copycats! This is why infants stick out their tongues in response to adults sticking out theirs. Until the discovery of mirror neurons, it was a total mystery how the infant would "know" that his tongue corresponds to the tongue of the adult. Although we can understand the adaptive purpose of this hard wiring (there is a survival advantage in feeling fear when those around us do), the contagion of emotions in a classroom can be disastrous in the moment-of-disruption. The most powerful tool we have in countering a negative contagion of emotions is controlling our own emotional reaction.

The *Win-Win Discipline* book describes numerous tools and strategies to help us control our emotions in the moment-of-disruption including: Teacher Think Time; Using a Calm Voice; I-Messages Plus; Modeling; and Scheduling a Follow-Up.

3. How can I teach student self-control?

In the face of aggression, safety is our first concern. Our second concern is being a positive model of self-control. Next, we help the aggressive student or students learn self-control.

The ABCD Questions

The *Win-Win Discipline* book includes a list of 26 Anger Control Techniques that can be employed by students to manage their own behavior and prevent aggressive displays of anger.

Structures that are helpful for student self-control include:

- **Implementing Preestablished Consequences:** *"We agreed if you choose to do X, the consequence would by Y. You did X, so we will implement Y."*
- **Language of Choice:** *"The respectful thing to do is work quietly on your project, or we will have a meeting after class to discuss this. It's your choice."*
- **Right-Now Validation:** *"Right now you are feeling angry. That's OK. The responsible thing to do is take a few slow, calm, deep breaths and then return to your desk and work on your project."*

B. Breaking the Rules

1. Does the student know the rule?

The three critical questions for Breaking the Rules address three levels of Bloom's Taxonomy. We start with checking for Knowledge, move to Comprehension, and then to Application. Does the student know what the rule is? If so, does the student comprehend the rule? And if so, can the student apply the rule to new situations? If the answer to any of these questions is no, we go into teaching mode, teaching for recall, comprehension, or application. Actively involving students in the formulation of rules and in discussion of their purpose helps ensure yes answers to the three questions and helps create buy-in as well.

Chapter 6: The ABCD Questions

If the student actually knows, understands, and can apply the rule but consciously chooses not to, the disruptive behavior is almost certainly a choice springing from one of the seven positions, and our response will depend on the student's position. For example, we respond differently to a student breaking the rules in order to establish a sense of control than a student breaking the rules for attention or out of anger toward the teacher.

Win-Win Discipline describes many ways to help students be aware of the rules, including:

- Keep Rules Simple
- One Rule
- T-Chart Rules
- Rule Poster
- Personal Rule Sheet
- Letter to Parents
- Clarify the Rule
- Model the Rule
- Pantomime the Rule
- Rule Mnemonics
- Multiple Intelligences Rule Reminders
- Illustrate the Rules
- Check for Understanding
- Teach and Re-Teach the Rules
- Collaboratively Create Rules

2. How can I promote understanding and buy-in?

Remembering a rule is not the same as understanding and identifying with the rule. Truly understanding a rule includes buying-in and accepting the need for the rule. Among the ways we promote understanding the rationale for rules and expectations in Win-Win are:

- Corroboratively Creating Rules and Expectations
- Students Teaching Rules
- Students Writing about Rule Purpose
- Asking "What Would Class Look Like without the Rule?"

The ABCD Questions

3. Can the student reliably apply the rule?

Understanding the necessity of driving a car carefully in icy conditions, is very different from *being able* to skillfully drive in icy conditions. Following rules on a consistent basis involves procedural knowledge. Procedural knowledge occurs in deeper, older areas of the brain. There is only one road to procedural knowledge: practice. Some students need more practice than others.

Among the ways we have students more consistently follow rules and live up to expectations are:

- Have Students Practice Rules
- Eliminate Temptations
- Provide Nonverbal Rule Cues
- Appreciate Rule Adherence
- Have Students Verbalize Responsible Behavior
- Teacher I-Messages or Affective Statements: *"When you do…, I feel…"*

C. Confrontation

1. Am I using self-control?

When a student confronts the teacher, either through active hostility or passive noncompliance, the first question for the teacher to ask is, "Am I controlling my reaction?" Some students are quite skilled at pushing teachers' buttons. If the teacher gets hooked (angry, sucked into a power play), then a Win-Win solution is impossible. To structure for a Win-Win solution, the teacher controls his or her own understandable frustration and anger, sidestepping the power play.

Chapter 6: The ABCD Questions

Among the ways we can control our own emotional reactions are:

- **Taking deep breaths**
- **Moving**
- **Talking more slowly**
- **Identifying with students' needs**
- **Validating student position**

Win-Win provides step-by-step structures that help us control our own emotional responses, including:

- **Schedule Follow-Up:** *"We need to talk this through. Let's meet after…"*
- **Table the Matter:** *"Let's give this a rest for now. We can talk about it later when we have both calmed down."*
- **To You… To Me:** *"To you, this lesson may be boring; to me, it is important because…"*

2. Can I provide the student with choices?

Confrontations are usually power plays: A student does not want to feel controlled or be told what to do. Students are less likely to oppose something they have chosen, so confrontations are reduced dramatically when we provide choices. Although we cannot allow students the choice of whether or not we will study math, we can allow choices about when it will be studied, which strategies we will use, and, to some extent, how students will demonstrate their understanding of the material. Sometimes

The ABCD Questions

in the moment of a confrontation, we can sidestep the confrontation by emphasizing that the student is in charge of deciding what they will or won't do, by using a structure, Acknowledge Student Power. For example, we might say, *"I can't make you do that assignment. If you choose to do it, you can raise your grade; if you choose not to do it, you will not earn any points. It is entirely your choice."*

Allowing choices in the moment of a confrontation is another way to diffuse the confrontation. For example, in response to a student who is refusing to do a worksheet or homework assignment we might say, *"If you do not want to solve the worksheet problems, you can choose to make up and solve your own pizza fraction problems."*

"If you would rather not answer the list of questions I have provided on colonial figures, you can choose among different options or suggest an option for my approval. Some possibilities include, choosing a figure of the times of your choice, then writing a dialogue between that figure and a modern figure, portraying that figure in a monologue, or creating an illustrated timeline of the most important events in your figure's life."

We reduce the probability of confrontations by giving students more choices on an ongoing basis. For examples, *"Students, today we can choose to study math in the morning or in the afternoon. What would you prefer?"*

"Today we can review using RallyCoach or Showdown. Each team will get to choose."

Chapter 6

The ABCD Questions

"Tomorrow we will conclude our study of the poems of Milton. To demonstrate your mastery of the unit, you have a choice: you can submit your own poem using stylistic elements we have studied, you can write an essay about the stylistic elements we have studied, or you can create a Mind Map of the stylistic elements with examples."

3. Am I using a Win-Win leadership style?

A Win-Win leadership style is a democratic leadership style. The Win-Win teacher solicits and respects student input. The students feel like part of the decision-making process, but they know that the teacher has final authority.

Elements of a Win-Win leadership style include:

- **The teacher shows respect for the needs and wishes of students.**
- **The teacher asks for student input on how to better run the class.**
- **Students and teacher cocreate discipline solutions.**
- **The teacher carves out areas of choice for students in curriculum and instruction.**
- **Minority opinions are respected.**
- **The dignity of each individual is maintained.**
- **Individual differences are celebrated.**
- **The feeling is same-side: "we" rather than "teacher vs. students."**

When a teacher assumes a Win-Win leadership style, students are far more likely to return the respect they are given.

The ABCD Questions

D. Disengagement

1. How can I reengage the student?

When students are not engaged in the learning process, we can reengage students by modifying the Big 3: Curriculum, Instruction, and Management. With relevant, developmentally appropriate curriculum, engaging instruction, and efficient management, disengagement is highly unlikely.

2. Is my curriculum engaging and relevant? Developmentally appropriate?

Students disengage if the curriculum is too easy or too difficult. Making our content developmentally appropriate is one path to engagement. Making the curriculum relevant to students' interests and needs is critical. Students are likely to disengage if they can't provide a positive answer to the question, *"How will learning this benefit me?"*

3. Is my instruction engaging? Am I using structures for engagement?

Disengagement is unlikely when engaging instructional strategies are used on a consistent basis. Students become more engaged when instruction includes:

- Choices
- Cooperative Learning
- Energizers
- Multiple Intelligences
- Novelty
- Relaxers
- Student Input
- Variety
- Visuals

Chapter 6: The ABCD Questions

4. Is my management engaging? Am I decreasing time off task?

Disengagement is reduced when management is efficient. In the *Win-Win Discipline* book, an entire chapter is dedicated to making management more efficient. Among the ways to tighten management are:

Learning Tasks
- Ready, Set, Go Work
- Staged Projects
- Clear Expectations/Goals

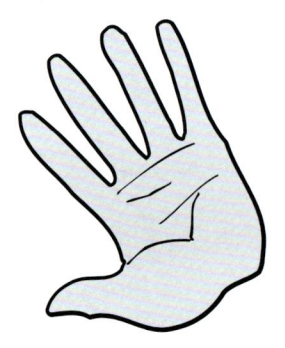

Signals and Signs
- Hand Signals
- Varied Signals
- Teach Timer
- Cues

Direction Giving
- Trigger Instructions
- Bite-Sized Instructions
- Concrete, Modeled Instructions
- Whisper

Simultaneous Management Techniques
- Simultaneous Response Modes
- Simultaneous Distribution of Materials
- Simultaneous Team Formation

Procedures
- Label Supplies
- Crisp Transitions
- Sponge Activities
- Team Questions: Three Before Me

The ABCD Questions

ABCD Questions – Helpful Guidelines

By asking and answering for ourselves simple disruption-specific ABCD questions, we are far better prepared to respond in moments-of-disruption in ways far more likely to create win-win solutions and foster learned responsibility.

For each of the four types of disruptions, there are critical questions. The questions are faithful guideposts, pointing toward responses appropriate to the disruption at hand. The questions compel us to look back: Have we emphasized enough the preventive procedures that might have eliminated the disruption? The questions also compel us to look at the moment-of-disruption: Do we need to address an immediate threat or to control our own reaction?

The questions, however, are only general direction posts; they are not full maps to a discipline solution. We cannot consistently formulate a successful Win-Win Discipline response by looking at behavior alone. The disruptive behavior is half the picture. The other half is the reason for the disruptive behavior, the position of the student. To ensure a successful Win-Win Discipline response, we must consider both behavior and position. It is to that second half of the equation, identifying the position of the student, which we turn in our next chapter.

Chapter 7

Identifying Positions

Chapter 7

Identifying Positions

The first step in formulating a Win-Win response to a disruption that ends the disruption and helps students learn responsibility is to identify the position of the student who is being disruptive. If the student is being disruptive because of a need for attention, we respond quite differently than if the student is being disruptive because he or she is angry.

Focusing on the position of the student, not just the disruptive behavior, gives us new eyes and we see our students very differently. Instead of a mean student, we see a student who has not learned responsible ways to deal with his or her anger. Instead of a disruptive class clown, we see a student who has not learned responsible ways to earn positive attention. Looking beyond behavior to position is like putting on a new pair of glasses!

Following their training in Win-Win Discipline, a remarkable number of teachers have commented that the program gives them "new eyes." They see each disruption differently, focusing not on the behavior itself but, rather, on the place from which it springs. A beginning teacher reported, *"By just looking for their position, it was easy to end disruptions. A bit of attention here, a choice there, a rule reminder over here, and my class was running more smoothly than ever."* When we look beyond behavior and see that the disruptions are only the consequence of unmet needs, the change in our approach to discipline is phenomenal. When we hone our skills of perception to see below the surface, positions begin to become remarkably clear. An experienced teacher reported, *"Win-Win Discipline is much bigger than a set of classroom strategies. It has changed the way I see friends, acquaintances, my family, and even myself!"*

Identifying Positions

Simply looking for student positions will carry you a long way. To determine a student's position, you have five clues in the moment-of-disruption and six strong indicators to use following the disruption.

Clues in the Moment-of-Disruption

In the moment-of-disruption, we have five clues to help us know a student's position:

1. Teacher Gut Reaction
2. Teacher Impulse
3. Disruptive Student's Reaction to Intervention
4. Classmates' Reactions to the Disruption
5. Student's Facial Expressions And Body Language

◆ **Clue 1: Teacher Gut Reaction.** Our gut reaction is our first clue. For example, if we look inside, we find we feel very different when a student is confronting us than when a student is seeking attention. When a student is confronting us, we feel challenged. We are likely to become defensive. We don't want someone taking over our class; we don't want a loss of control in front of the whole class. If the student is strong or is being successful in his or her play for power or control, we might feel threatened.

In contrast, our reaction is quite different toward the student who is seeking attention. In some ways it is almost the opposite. Whereas our gut tells us the control-seeking student wants to take something from us (our power, our control), the attention-seeking students want us to give them something (our attention, ultimately, our love). We feel drained. If the attention seeking continues, we become irritated and annoyed.

Chapter 7

Identifying Positions

Each of us carries with us a great internal position detector—our gut reactions. Our most common gut reaction to each position is listed in the table: Clues to Student Positions found at the end of this section, on page 73. That table lists all five clues for each position.

◆ **Clue 2: Teacher Impulses.** Whereas your gut reactions are feelings, your impulses are impetus toward actions. When I watch Peter hit Hal for no apparent reason, I feel protective toward Hal and angry toward Peter. Those are feelings. My impulses are to hug or comfort or protect Hal in some other way and to punish or let Peter know he cannot hurt other students without consequences in some other way.

My impulses toward action are my second clue for determining position. Our impulses toward students are a response to their position. When Matt gets out of his chair for the fourth time this hour, I have the impulse to pick him up and tape him down to his chair! Jennifer's incessant tapping of her pencil makes me want to grab the pencil away! These impulses to suppress behavior are a clue that I am reacting to students coming from a position of energy. When their energy disrupts the class, I have the impulse to suppress it.

My impulsive reaction to an energetic student is quite in contrast to my impulsive reaction to a student in a position of boredom. When a student is bored, I feel invalidated (my lesson is not working) and have the impulse to engage the student in some way or to focus on other students who are engaged, discounting or ignoring the bored student.

Identifying Positions

When a student is socially uninformed, my impulse is to help or inform him or her, but if I have done that many times to no avail, I might have the impulse to ignore the student.

Tuning in to our impulses is the second internal barometer we have for detecting student position. The remaining clues and indicators are external. They involve observing others or soliciting their input.

◆ Clue 3: Disruptive Student's Reaction to Intervention

If we watch the disruptive student carefully as we intervene, the student reveals his or her position. The student seeking attention gets more relaxed when attention is given, but if the student is ignored, he or she tries harder for attention or tries in a different way. Ignoring students seeking attention is a sure way to drive them to new heights in their search for what they need. A slight smile appears when the need is met, and pouting, frowning, or intensified action appears when the need goes unmet.

The student who punches a classmate out of anger responds to intervention quite differently than the student who punches because of excess energy or playfulness. When the teacher prohibits the behavior, the angry student might sulk; the playful student might smile. In one case, satisfaction of the need has been interrupted; in the other case, the need has been satisfied.

◆ Clue 4: Classmates' Reactions to the Disruption

Classmates react quite differently to disruptions springing from different positions. Carlos catches the teacher in an error and points it out in front of the whole class. If Carlos is coming from a position of attention-seeking

Chapter 7

Identifying Positions

(look at me; aren't I clever?), the class is likely to be amused. If Carlos is constantly contradicting the teacher in an attempt to get attention, the class will become irritated with him ("there goes Carlos, *again*").

If, however, Carlos is coming from a position of seeking control ("I'm smarter than you, I can teach the class"), the class is not amused or irritated. They back off. They sense a power play in progress. There will be a struggle for control. They become very watchful, wondering who will come out on top. This watchful orientation during a struggle is quite in contrast to the amused or irritated response that says, "There goes Carlos trying to be cute again."

◆ **Clue 5. Student's Facial Expressions and Body Language** Each of the positions is associated with needs that are expressed in the face and body. The angry face is universally recognized, even among primitive people who have had no contact with written words or Western ways. Darwin was the first to systematically record what the eyes, eyebrows, nose, lips, jaw, and facial muscles do when one experiences different emotions, and his observations have held true and extend even to nonhuman primates.

Identifying Positions

Clues to Student Positions (In the Moment-of-Disruption)

Student Position	Teacher Gut Reaction	Teacher Impulse	Disruptive Student's Reaction to Intervention	Classmate Reactions to the Disruption	Student's Facial Expressions; Body Language
Attention-Seeking	Drained, irritated, annoyed	Nag, scold	Temporary compliance	Amused, irritated	Catching an eye; Looking up
Avoiding Failure	Sympathetic, protective, challenged, helpless	Tutor; Give up, write off	Feigns lack of interest; "I can't"; Half-hearted effort	Resentment, pity	Avoiding eye contact; Low muscle tone
Angry	Threatened, fearful, protective, indignant, outraged	Remove, punish, retaliate	Anger, revenge-seeking, sulking	Fearful, angry	Jaw protrudes; Eyebrows lowered and drawn; Lips pressed; Fist clenched
Control-Seeking	Challenged, angry, threatened, frustrated	Force compliance; Put down; Overpower; Fight	Get in the "last word"; Power plays; Argue, Justify	Defiance, deference	Crossed arms; Tightly closed lips; Pointing; Staring; Puffed up; Loud
Bored	Invalidated	Discount; Engage	Off task	Reject, ignore	Low muscle tone; Droopy eyes
Energetic	Overwhelmed, exhausted, drained	Suppress	Continues, increases, modifies activity; Playful smile	Distraction, annoyance, envy	High muscle tone; Animated movement
Socially Uninformed	Pity, helpful, exasperated, impatient	Help, inform, ignore	Grateful; Lack of understanding; Obedient	Annoyance, pity, impatience	Surprise; Wide eyed; Lowered head

Win-Win Discipline
Kagan Publishing • 800.933.2667 • www.KaganOnline.com

Identifying Positions

Beyond the Clues: Indicators

The five clues are available to us in the moment-of-disruption. Following the disruption, we can use six indicators to help us infer a student's position. The Indicators are:

1. **Interviews with Disruptive Student**
2. **Student's Reaction to Interventions**
3. **Interviews with Classmates**
4. **Interviews with Prior Teachers**
5. **Interviews with Parents**
6. **Cumulative Charts**

Details of obtaining and using these indicators are presented in the book *Win-Win Discipline*.

Positions Are Independent of Behaviors

When we see a student hit another student, it is natural to assume the disruptive student is angry. In fact, however, the aggressive student might be attention-seeking from peers, trying to establish dominance or control, attempting to distract attention from not being able to do a task, trying to let off some excess energy, unaware of the appropriate behavior in school, or simply bored and wanting to get some action going.

We can never infer position by just observing behavior. Any behavior can spring from almost any position. To infer position, we need to use the clues and indicators. We need to look beyond behavior.

Chapter 8

Validating Positions

Chapter 8
Validating Positions

Having identified a student position, the Win-Win teacher finds a variety of ways to communicate to the student the following message:

Although I find your disruptive behavior unacceptable, I understand and fully accept your position.

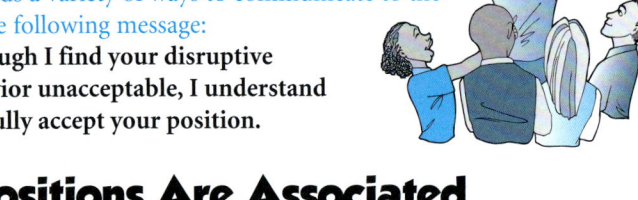

Positions Are Associated with Basic Needs

Student positions are associated with basic human needs. For example, Attention-Seeking is an attempt to feel cared about, appreciated by others. Control-Seeking is an attempt to have an impact on others and events. It is associated also with the need not to be controlled by others. The Socially Uninformed position differs from the other six positions. Disruptive behavior stemming from the Socially Uninformed position is not a disruptive attempt to satisfy a need; rather, disruptive behavior springing from the Socially Uninformed position stems from a lack of understanding of internalization and consistent adherence to school behavior norms.

- **Attention-Seeking:** To feel cared about by others
- **Avoiding Failure:** To feel successful
- **Angry:** To express displeasure
- **Control-Seeking:** To feel able to influence people and events
- **Energetic:** To move, touch, be expressive
- **Bored:** To be motivated, to have interesting stimuli
- **Socially Uninformed:** To know how to behave in a social setting

There is never anything wrong with being in a position or having the needs associated with that position. What can be disruptive, though, is

Validating Positions

what a student does to meet those needs. By validating the position of the student, the teacher lays the groundwork for a Win-Win solution to the discipline problem. By validating the student's position, the student feels supported by the teacher and is more open to seeking responsible, nondisruptive ways to meet his or her needs.

The Win-Win teacher validates student positions for a number of reasons:

1. When a student feels validated, a basic need is met and he or she relaxes, becoming less likely to be disruptive.
2. When a student feels validated, he or she likes the teacher more and is more open to input, becoming more compliant.
3. Feeling validated by the teacher, the student wants to please the teacher.
4. Feeling validated for who he or she is, an otherwise disruptive student no longer needs to be disruptive because the disruptive behavior was merely a misguided attempt to win acceptance.
5. If the student does not feel accepted by the teacher, the student is likely to become more disruptive out of anger. "If you reject me, I will reject you."
6. When we validate a student's position, we create a bridge for that student—a bridge toward self-knowledge and self-acceptance. Feeling his or her position is known and accepted by the teacher, the student can better know and accept it. The teacher actually models an orientation toward the student that the student can internalize. And until the student knows and accepts his or her own position, the student will continue to act out the needs of the position rather than consider responsible alternatives.

Chapter 8: Validating Positions

Paradox 1: Win-Lose Becomes Lose-Lose

The starting point toward a Win-Win solution, is to accept and validate student positions. If we reject student positions, we are headed for a Win-Lose solution. In a Win-Lose discipline solution, the teacher suppresses the disruptive behavior, but the student does not get his or her needs met. A Win-Lose solution is a prescription for another disruption down the road. Following a Win-Lose solution, unmet needs simmer, eventually boiling over into another disruption. Thus, paradoxically, in the long run there is never a Win-Lose; short-run Win-Lose solutions become long-run Lose-Lose outcomes.

Paradox 2: Self-Acceptance Leads to Change

Validating the student position helps communicate that we are on the same-side as the student. Through validation, we let students know we accept and care about them. Feeling this, the student is more likely to accept himself or herself. Change is possible only when we recognize where we are; if we expend our energy in denial, we are stuck, and change is unlikely. Here we have a second paradox: self-acceptance leads to change.

I understand you...

Validating Student Positions

Nonverbal Validation

We can validate a student's position nonverbally with a smile, a gesture, a nod, a look, or a gentle hand on his or her shoulder. There is a simple technique that allows us to communicate to students that we accept their position without saying a word!

Validating Positions

What is the trick? Experts estimate that about 80% of human communication is nonverbal. Our face, body position, muscle tensions, breathing rate and volume, and even our heart field communicate worlds to those around us. That is why young children and animals have accurate instinctive positive or negative reactions toward a stranger, even before the person says a word.

How then can we use this unconscious communication to transmit to our students a message of acceptance of their basic position? Remember this:

We almost always communicate what we feel, whether we intend to or not.

So, the trick is simple:
To communicate acceptance of positions, all we have to do is feel acceptance of positions.

Validation Phrases

The second way we can validate student positions are gambits, phrases that communicate knowledge and acceptance of the student's position.

Attention-Seeking
"We all need approval sometimes. It felt really good to me yesterday when a student told me she enjoyed the lesson. I bet you would feel great if you aced this test."

Avoiding Failure
"None of us wants to fail. Let's practice these problems in our teams now so when we do this type of problem on the homework alone tonight, we will be sure to get them all right."

Chapter 8

Validating Positions

Angry
"All of us feel angry when we feel we have been treated unfairly. Certainly, I did not want to treat you unfairly. Let's review what happened."

Control-Seeking
"None of us wants to be told what to do all the time. For that reason, tonight you will have a choice between two types of homework. You get to decide."

Bored
"Well, all of us get bored sometimes. How can we make this more interesting for you?"

Energetic
"You are full of energy today! Let's see if we can work together to channel that energy into some productive learning."

Socially Uninformed
"I can see how you did not remember the rules. That happens to all of us sometimes. Let's work together to figure out a way to make them easier for you to remember."

Validation Promotes a Same-Side Orientation

Student validation is the Same-Side pillar in action. When we acknowledge and accept students' positions, we take the side of our students and communicate that we understand and accept them. We couple this acceptance of their position, however, with a clear message that we do not accept their disruptive behavior. By communicating an acceptance of the student's position and a rejection of the student's behavior, we build two kinds of bridges.

Validating Positions

First, validation builds a bridge between the student and ourself. I am no different from you; I, too, sometimes get angry, antsy, or bored. When the student feels his or her position is accepted (even if the teacher will not accept the disruptive behavior), when the student knows the teacher identifies with him or her, the student reciprocates, identifying with the teacher. Care becomes mutual, and the student is less motivated to disrupt the teacher's class and more motivated to want to help the teacher. When the student feels rejected, the student is more likely to strike back with disruptive behavior; when the student feels accepted, the student is more likely to reciprocate with positive behavior.

The second bridge is within the student. Validation of student position builds a bridge to student self-knowledge. The disruptive student often is out of touch with his or her own position. The student acts out his or her anger or boredom or excess energy often without being aware of his or her position and needs. Until the student knows his or her position, the student is destined to act it out. Validation from the teacher is like holding up a mirror—the student then begins to understand and be accepting.

Receiving consistent validation from the teacher, the student internalizes the validation and begins to adopt a new attitude: "I am OK. There is nothing wrong with me. My behavior has not been acceptable, but I am liked, cared for, and accepted."

Chapter 8

Validating Positions

From this attitude of self-acceptance and self-liking flows a number of benefits: the student experiences improved self-esteem, confidence, and acceptance of others. The student distinguishes himself or herself from the behavior and realizes it is possible to maintain his or her identity while changing his or her behavior.

Until we feel accepted, in contact with ourselves, we do not have the knowledge or courage to change. Validation builds the self-knowledge and self-acceptance necessary for change.

Chapter 9

Responding to the Seven Positions

Chapter 9

Responding to the Seven Positions

If we have put in place what has been described so far in this mini-book, we have put in place our behavior-based and position-based preventive procedures. That eliminated most of our discipline problems. Further, in the moment-of-disruption, we have asked the critical ABCD questions and responded accordingly. Although we now face far fewer disruptions and are responding appropriately to different types of disruptions, there remains the question of how best to respond in the moment-of-disruption to each of the seven student positions.

Ideally, in the moment-of-disruption, we would achieve five goals:

1. **Quickly end the disruption and minimize the missed instructional time for all students.**
2. **Communicate that the disruptive behavior is unacceptable.**
3. **Communicate validation of the student position.**
4. **Communicate a Win-Win orientation, a willingness to team up and seek mutually beneficial solutions.**
5. **Foster long-term learning of autonomous responsible behaviors.**

The *Win-Win Discipline* book offers many ways to respond to each of the seven positions. Each of these ideas is described in the book. Here, we will just list the ideas to provide an overview of some of the tools we have to respond to each position.

Responding to the Seven Positions

Attention-Seeking

Moment-of-disruption strategies for attention-seeking fall into two opposite categories: those designed to communicate that disruptive behavior is not a way to get attention and those designed to fill the need for attention. It is only when the student is not being disruptive that we attempt to reinforce responsible ways of seeking attention. Among the ways to respond to attention-seeking:

- Hand Signals
- Physical Touch
- Private Written Note
- Proximity
- Student's Name in an Example
- Give Jobs, Tasks
- Assign Roles

Avoiding Failure

We all need to feel successful and want to avoid failures, especially public failures that can lead to embarrassment. Avoiding failure helps us preserve our self-respect and our status within the group. It is much less painful to say to oneself and others, "I didn't care, so I didn't try," than to say, "I really cared a lot and tried my hardest but failed anyway." So avoiding failure is protection for our ego.

Chapter 9: Responding to the Seven Positions

Among the ways to respond to avoiding failure:

- **Appreciation**
- **Bite-Sized Instructions**
- **Cooperative Structures**
- **RallyCoach**
- **Team-Pair-Solo**
- **Numbered Heads Together**
- **Encouragement**
- **Multiple Intelligences Instruction**
- **Multiple Intelligences Encourager**
- **Monitor and Adjust**
- **Peer Tutoring**
- **Private Feedback Reminder**
- **Practice Retribution**
- **Teacher Tutoring**
- **Share Fears**

Angry

We all get angry at times. Anger is a natural biological response to frustration and threat. Anger helps us survive; it prepares us to avoid threats and signals others not to threaten us. We all know the student who is picked on mercilessly until that student finally displays anger, and then the others back off. Students need to learn that their anger is never the problem, but what they do when angry can be a problem. There are different ways of "handling" anger—some responsible and others disruptive.

In the moment of an anger-based disruption, sometimes all we can do is get the angry student to calm down. Sometimes, though, the angry outburst is not so prolonged or severe, in which case we can guide the student to explore nondisruptive ways of handling anger.

Responding to the Seven Positions

To help students calm down, we have a variety of options, including catharsis, distraction, reciprocal inhibition, transfer, and teaching and modeling alternatives. If the anger is strong enough, we may need to have the student leave the situation that produced the anger.

The *Win-Win Discipline* book details the following ways to help students who are angry:

Catharsis
- Draw It Out
- Mold It
- Talk It Out
- Write It Out
- Choice
- Exercise
- The Tetherball

Distraction
- Guided Imagery
- Leave the Field
- Perspective Shift
- Induction

Reciprocal Inhibition
- Concentration
- Think Time: Student
- Food
- Humor

Transfer
- Academic Content

Teach, Model Positive Alternatives
- Reminder: STOP HACC*
- Replacement Reminder
- Think Time: Teacher
- Class Meeting
- Peer Mediation

* **Eight modes of conflict resolution:** S=Share, T=Take Turns, O=Outside, P=Postpone, H=Humor, A=Avoid, C=Compromise, C=Chance

Chapter 9

Responding to the Seven Positions

Control-Seeking

To feel that what we do makes a difference, that we are in control of ourselves and the things around us, is a basic need. Those who lose their sense of control fall into depression. With complete loss of the sense of control, people actually give up and die with no physical ailments.[1] Therefore, we want to support our students' drive to exert control. Obtaining and maintaining a sense of control is part of what it is to be healthy.

Like all needs, however, the drive for a sense of control can play out in disruptive behaviors. When that happens, we want to make sure the student knows the disruption is not acceptable, but that the drive for control is healthy.

Among the ways to respond to a student who is control-seeking:

- **Calm Consequences**
- **Choices**
- **Humor**
- **Owning Choices**
- **Sidestep the Power Play**
- **Plus/Minus T-Chart**

Bored

Boredom is a physiological state. It involves low stimulation in two areas of the brain: attention and motivation. The opposite of boredom is intense concentration and high motivation.

Recent research has shown that the increased attention and motivation most people feel as a result of drinking a cup of coffee is due to increased dopamine in the brain. Dopamine stimu-

Responding to the Seven Positions

lates the brain's attention and motivation centers. Ritalin prompts hyperactive students to concentrate and finish tasks in the same way, stimulating the attention and motivation centers, but with much higher doses. Some hyperactive, inattentive students become attentive and motivated when Ritalin takes effect.

In this set of findings is a partial answer to the question of what to do in the moment-of-disruption when a student is disruptive due to boredom. The bored student may be is daydreaming, doodling, or looking around at everything but the task at hand. When asked, the student says the task is dumb. When we delve a bit deeper, we find that the student is not interested in the task and has no motivation to complete it. The student is in the position of boredom.

What can we do in the moment-of-disruption when a student is disruptive due to boredom, becoming disengaged and/or distracting others? The Win-Win first response is not to buy the student a cup of coffee or to dose the student with Ritalin. Our first response is to examine our curriculum, instruction, and management techniques in the moment-of-disruption to attempt to make them more motivating and interesting. This is not to say that Ritalin is always inappropriate; it is to say that a great deal of inattentiveness springs from curriculum and instruction which is not interesting and/or motivating for students. The first place we look, therefore, if we are seeking a Win-Win solution to deal with boredom, is making our teaching more engaging. We have presented ways to increase engagement in **Chapter 3: Preventing ABCD Disruptions** (page 25) and in **Chapter 5: Preventing Position-Based Disruptions** (page 43).

Chapter 9: Responding to the Seven Positions

The long-term goal is to have students become self-motivated and self-engaging. The place to start, though, is by supporting motivation and engagement via how and what we teach.

Among the ways to respond to a student who is bored:

- **Cooperative Learning**
- **Curriculum Shift**
- **Developmentally Appropriate Curriculum**
- **Dramatic Reopeners**
- **Energizers**
- **Instruction Shift**
- **Intelligence Shift**
- **Interest Links**
- **Name Dropping**
- **Relevance**
- **Simultaneous Response Modes**

Energetic

Energy is a gift. Many of the great contributors to mankind have had what seems like boundless energy. We want students to realize that having a high level of energy doesn't make someone abnormal; it is to be desired. The basic need to move, touch, manipulate things, interact, and be expressive is a gift which prompts us to know and understand, create and invent, relate and care. The energy of students is never the problem.

Of course, like any gift, energy can be used in responsible or disruptive ways. We are all too familiar with the student who just can't seem to sit still, who cannot keep his or her hands off

Responding to the Seven Positions

everything and everyone, and who has to be restrained from nonstop talking. The challenge for the Win-Win teacher is to accept the energy of the student, reject disruptive behavior, and help the student learn to channel the energy in positive directions. Unchanneled energy detracts from learning—for the energetic student and those around him or her. In the extreme cases, students with a great deal of unchanneled energy receive the label of ADHD, Attention Deficit Hyperactivity Disorder. Students who have learned to channel their energy in responsible ways receive the label High Achiever.

Among the ways to respond to a student who is energetic:

Energy Releases
- Energizers
- Exercise
- Roles and Responsibilities
- Silly Sports & Goofy Games

Calming Strategies
- Calm Curriculum
- Music at 60 Beats per Minute
- Progressive Relaxation
- Relaxation Breathing
- Removing Distractions
- Visualization
- Guided Imagery
- Mental Retreats

Channeling Energy Productively
- Bite-Sized Instruction
- Channel Energy
- Classbuilders
- Curriculum Shift
- Instruction Shift
- Multiple Intelligences: Bodily/Kinesthetic Instruction
- Sponge

Chapter 9: Responding to the Seven Positions

Socially Uninformed

In some ways, a student in the socially uninformed position is the easiest of all to deal with; in other ways, the socially uninformed student is the most difficult.

It is easy because the disruption is not motivated by a strongly held emotion. When a student is very angry or passionately seeking control, he or she is highly motivated to express anger or demonstrate control. So, to end the disruption, we are opposing a great deal of drive. In contrast, when a student simply does not know, it is simply a lack of information, skill, or habit. There is no drive to be socially uninformed and thus no resistance to overcome. In fact, we have drive on our side—there is a human drive to know and understand.

The socially uninformed position, though, can be the most difficult and frustrating of all. The class has agreed on a rule. We have made the rule clear, given the rationale for the rule, demonstrated the rule, practiced the rule, had students make up ways to remember the rule—in short, we've done all it seems possible to do. Then a student once again breaks the rule. At that point, our initial impulse is to give up.

In the moment-of-disruption, we need to be sure the student is truly socially uninformed. The student's reaction to intervention is usually our best clue. A student walks into

Responding to the Seven Positions

the room late or without the required materials. When we do a rule reminder, the student says, "Oh! I forgot." But how does the student say it? What is the tone? What is the body language of the student? Does the student act surprised by our rule reminder, or does the student act as if caught at something he or she was trying to get away with? Does the student give a sly smile indicating he or she knew the teacher would see, revealing the disruption is a bid for attention? We gather all the clues we can. Is the student really in the socially uninformed position?

It does not matter how many times we have taught and retaught a rule. The student is socially uninformed in the moment-of-disruption if he or she truly does not remember the rule or knows the rule but does not yet adhere to it. Ultimately, the truly socially uninformed position is an innocent position. It is a lack of learning. Our tools are the same as when a student doesn't grasp our academic content. We remotivate the learning, we teach it again in a different way, and we work with the student to discover what works for that student to produce learning.

As frustrating as the socially uninformed position can be, if we can discover a way for the student to become informed, we have probably discovered a path to greater learning in the academic areas as well. The ultimate goal in working with the socially uninformed student is fostering the ability to learn how to learn.

Chapter 9: Responding to the Seven Positions

Among the ways to respond to a student who is socially uninformed:

- **Classroom Buddies**
- **Cooperative Learning**
- **Draw Attention to a Positive Model**
- **Reflection Time; Improvement Plan**
- **Proximity**
- **Rule Reminder**

Reference

[1] Seligman, M. *Helplessness: On Depression, Development, and Death.* San Francisco, CA: W.H. Freeman and Company, 1975.

Chapter 10

Moment-of-Disruption Structures

Chapter 10: Moment-of-Disruption Structures

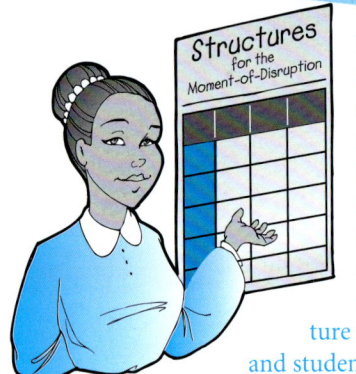

In the emergency of a moment-of-disruption, it is best to have specific, step-by-step sequences to run off. The more we use these Win-Win strategies, the more we can remain calm and effective in the moment-of-disruption. In the Win-Win Discipline program, we call these structured teacher response structures. Why? Because they structure the interaction between the teacher and student(s) in predictable ways aligned with the philosophy and goal of Win-Win Discipline. They make it more likely the teacher can efficiently end the disruption, and the student will learn more responsible ways to meet the needs associated with his or her position.

In *Win-Win Discipline,* 20 moment-of-disruption structures are presented to help teachers respond to the ABCD behaviors and the seven student positions. In this mini-book, we feature four moment-of-disruption structures:

- **Make a Better Choice**
- **Language of Choice**
- **I-Messages Plus**
- **Table the Matter**

Moment-of-Disruption Structures

The four selected structures have different functions:

◆ **Make a Better Choice** puts the responsibility on an individual or the class as a whole to reflect on their own behavior and to decide on a more responsible, less disruptive behavior. The structure is aligned with the Win-Win philosophy because it calls for a collaborative solution. Rather than just demanding obedience, students choose more responsible behavior, subject to teacher approval. By putting the responsibility on the students to come up with the responsible behavior, we are closer to learned responsibility than if the teacher were to tell the students how to behave.

The essence of Make a Better Choice is captured by the teacher's gambit: *"You are disrupting your classmates and interfering with my ability to teach. Please make a better choice right now."*

◆ **Language of Choice** is used when we want to put pressure on students to be more responsible. The teacher stacks the cards in favor of students making a more responsible choice by making the alternative less desirable. Although the teacher poses the language as a choice, the teacher has made the responsible behavior more attractive than the alternative.

Chapter 10: Moment-of-Disruption Structures

The essence of Language of Choice is captured by the teacher providing the student a choice between responsible behavior and a less attractive alternative. For example, the teacher might say, *"You can put your doodling away and resume work on your assignment, or we can have a conference after class today."*

◆ **I-Messages Plus** calmly informs students how their behavior is disruptive to the teacher or others and encourages them to adopt a nondisruptive alternative. By directing the attention of the disruptive student to the impact of his or her behavior on others, I-Messages Plus fosters empathy and decreases the probability of future disruptions. Going forward, students are more sensitive to how their behavior impacts others.

The essence of I-Messages Plus is captured by the teacher's gambit: *"When you do [disruptive behavior], I feel [teacher's feelings] and your classmates feel [students' feelings]. Can you think of a better choice?"* For example, the teacher might say, *"When you make fun of the lesson, I feel frustrated because I want everyone to know how important this is, and your classmates feel distracted from learning. Can you think of a better choice?"*

Moment-of-Disruption Structures

◆ **Table the Matter** puts a respectful end to a confrontation. Some students want to go on and on arguing a point like arguing for a better grade. A prolonged confrontation generates escalating emotions in both the teacher and the student. When we see there is no end in sight to a debate, we can use Table the Matter to respectfully end the confrontation without putting the student down or giving in.

The essence of Table the Matter is captured by the teacher's gambit: *"Let's give this a rest for now. We can talk about it when we are both calm."*

Chapter 10: Moment-of-Disruption Structures

Make a Better Choice

Through Make a Better Choice, the teacher calls for reflection rather than obedience, leaving it to the student to create a more responsible alternative. *"I want you to think of a better choice you could make right now."*

Ideal Outcomes

- Students create solutions and do not feel like pawns.
- There is greater shared responsibility for the solution.
- Students internalize the reflective process.
- Students make more autonomous responsible choices.
- Students engage in creative thinking.
- Pressure on the teacher is lessened.

Recommended for...
Disruption: Aggression, Breaking the Rules, Disengagement
Position: Attention-Seeking, Avoiding Failure, Angry, Control-Seeking, Energetic, Bored
Individual or Class: Both

Moment-of-Disruption Structures

Make a Better Choice

Steps

1. Stop!
The teacher tells the student to stop disruptive behavior. *"Catherine, you need to stop throwing food."*

"Class, everyone stop what you are doing right now."

2. Think!
The teacher tells the student to think of better choices. *"Catherine, I want you to think of a better choice you could be making right now."*

"Class, I want each of you to think of a better choice you could make."

3. Please Tell!
The teacher asks the student to verbalize his or her better choices. *"Catherine, please tell me. What is your better choice?"*

"Class, I want each of you to turn to your shoulder partner and share both ways. What is your better choice?"

4. Agree and Act or Disagree and Request Better Choices
The teacher paraphrases the "better choice" and expresses agreement or lack of agreement. *"Catherine, your better choice is to clean up the mess and not to throw food in the cafeteria again. [pause] I agree. Thank you. That is responsible thinking. Please make your better choice now."*

"Catherine, your better choice is to leave the cafeteria right now. [pause] I don't agree, because that would leave the mess for others to clean up. I think you can come up with a better choice yet. What is a better choice?"

"Class, I heard some great choices. Some of the things I heard were _____, _____, and _____. Thank you for your responsible thinking. Now let's align our actions with our thoughts."

Cautions & Hints
- **Make It Private.** Work with students in private if possible.
- **Think Time.** Allow students sufficient time to think of their "better choice." Ideally, you maintain patience waiting until they come up with the choice on their own.
- **Written Choice.** If a student needs more time, in some circumstances you may ask the student to sit and write or draw the better choice.
- **Compliment Students.** Appreciate students for their "Responsible Thinking."

Chapter 10

Moment-of-Disruption Structures

Language of Choice

Language of choice provides immediate consequences, allowing the disruptive student to make a more responsible choice. *"Your choice is _____ or _____."*

Ideal Outcomes

- The student is oriented toward the responsible alternative.

- The student is prompted to reflect on the consequences of his or her actions.

- Loss of instructional time is kept to a minimum.

- Expectations of responsible behavior are communicated to the student.

- The teacher is more easily able to control his or her reaction.

- The teacher is provided with a frame for a quick response in the face of disruptive behavior.

Recommended for...

Disruption: Aggression, Breaking the Rules, Confrontation, Disengagement
Position: Attention-Seeking, Angry, Control-Seeking, Energetic, Bored, Socially Uninformed
Individual or Class: Both

Moment-of-Disruption Structures

Language of Choice

1. Validate Student or Position

This step solidifies an empathetic understanding of the student. When the teacher lets a student know they are on the Same-Side, positive results can follow. *"There is nothing wrong with getting upset when you make mistakes on the computer..."*

"If I haven't mentioned it lately, you are such a great asset to our class..."

2. State Responsible Behavior (*"The responsible choice is _____."*)

The teacher states the specific responsible behavior that the student needs to be exhibiting. *"The responsible choice is to use the computer keys appropriately and stop banging on them."*

"The responsible choice is to stand in line with your hands to your side."

Note: Avoid saying *"I need you to…"* or *"I want you to…"* as this provokes confrontation. Instead, say *"The responsible choice is…"*

3. State Consequences (*"or _____"*)

The teacher then states what the consequence (cool-down time, loss of privilege) will be if the student does not choose the responsible behavior. *"…or you can do the worksheet problems by hand."*

"…or you will need to go to the end of the line."

4. It's Your Choice

The teacher emphasizes that it is the student's option to choose the responsible behavior or the consequence. *"It is your choice: you can choose to use the computer or not."*

5. Encouragement

The teacher encourages the student to choose the responsible behavior. *"I'm sure you can make a responsible choice."*

6. If Nonverbal, Noncompliance

"It is evident by your actions and/or behavior that you have chosen to do the worksheet problems by hand. Is that correct?"

Chapter 10: Moment-of-Disruption Structures

Language of Choice (continued)

Cautions & Hints

- **Use Sparingly.** Language of Choice does not involve the student in creating the solution.
- **Attractive Choices.** By giving attractive choices, you make it easier for the student to choose a responsible alternative.
- **Private.** When possible, use Language of Choice without an audience. An audience can be an incentive to "not back down." It is easier to switch to responsible behavior if peers are not watching/listening.
- **Stopgap.** Language of Choice is a quick intervention orienting the student to what he or she is doing and causing the student to take responsibility for the consequences of his or her actions. Nevertheless, it is not a Win-Win solution because it does not involve students proposing alternatives—shared responsibility for the solutions. If you find yourself using Language of Choice often with a student, it may be time for a Responsible Thinking follow-up.
- **Counter-Indicated in Confrontation.** In the heat of a confrontation, Language of Choice can backfire, feeding a confrontation. During a "You can't make me" confrontation, Language of Choice will likely lead to an irresponsible choice because the student is bent on proving that the teacher can't get him or her to make the responsible choice. In the midst of a heated confrontation, the teacher is better off choosing Cool Down, Model It!, I-Messages, or a structure that does not force a choice.
- **Soft Tone.** If the disruption does not call for a forceful response, Language of Choice can be used with a soft tone: *"Please use the science equipment appropriately or you will lose the use of the equipment for today."*

Moment-of-Disruption Structures

Language of Choice (continued)

Cautions & Hints (continued)

- **Calm Voice.** Even if a student is being confrontational, only use Language of Choice if you think the student is likely to choose the responsible alternative. Take a moment to take a deep breath, pause, and consider carefully what you will say following the "or" of Language of Choice. Then use Language of Choice in a calm voice.
- **No False Threats.** To maintain credibility when using Language of Choice, whatever comes after the "or" must be something you are willing to follow through with.
- **Avoiding Loss.** Language of Choice is a stop structure, whereas Grandma's Rule is a start structure. With Grandma's Rule, we make salient the incentive for finishing a task; with Language of Choice, we make salient the loss which will result from persisting in disruptive behavior. With Grandma's Rule, the teacher uses a *"When… then…"* statement to indicate the responsible behavior and the incentive that will follow. *"When you do X… then you get Y."* Grandma's Rule is a Moment-of-Disruption structure. The steps of Grandma's Rule are in *Win-Win Discipline,* chapter 14.
- **Emphasize the Positive.** The emphasis should be on the positive side of the equation, not on the potential loss. OK: *"I'm sure you can return to your seat so we do not have to schedule a meeting with your parents to discuss this."* Not OK: *"If you don't return to your seat, I will be calling your parents to discuss this."*
- **Responsible Thinking and Responsible Behavior Follow-Ups:** If you find yourself using Language of Choice with a student frequently, the student is not internalizing the process. It is time then for a follow-up focused on Responsible Thinking or Responsible Behavior.

Chapter 10: Moment-of-Disruption Structures

I-Messages Plus

Calmly informing students of your own feelings is an "I-Message" designed to make students aware of their stimulus value (effect on others). I-Messages Plus adds encouragement to adopt a nondisruptive alternative. *"I feel X when you do Y, and your classmates feel Z. Can you think of a better choice?"*

Ideal Outcomes

- The student becomes more aware of his or her "stimulus value" – the effect he or she is having on others.

- I-Messages shift from authoritarian "right-wrong" to "person-to-person" relationships.

- I-Messages shift from blame ("you did") to information ("When you do x, I feel y").

- Emphasis is placed on specific behaviors, paving the way for change.

- The student can empathize with the teacher and others.

- The teacher maintains a calm, centered position.

- I-Messages provide a tight frame that allows quick, focused feedback to the disruptive student.

- Using I-Messages, the teacher can avoid escalation of emotion. It helps prevent the disruptive student from feeling rejected.

Recommended for...

Disruption: Aggression, Breaking the Rules, Disengagement
Position: Attention-Seeking, Avoiding Failure, Angry, Control-Seeking, Energetic, Bored, Socially Uninformed
Individual or Class: Both

Moment-of-Disruption Structures

I-Messages Plus

1. Validate the Position
The teacher starts with a validation of the student. *"Sean, I understand you would like to share…"*

"Bob, I know this assignment is not the most interesting for you…"

2. State How the Disruption Makes You Feel
The teacher states the impact of the disruptive behavior with a "… but I feel _____ when you _____ " statement. *"…but I feel annoyed when you talk while others are sharing."*

3. Describe the Effect of Disruptive Behavior on Classmates
The teacher states the effect the disruptive behavior has on others. *"If you talk while Trish is sharing, others cannot hear her. It is not polite to Trish. It is her turn. You would not want others to interrupt your turn."*

4. Redirect to Responsible Behavior to Meet Needs
The teacher helps the student commit to more responsible alternatives that would meet the student's needs without being disruptive. *"What are things you could choose that would allow you to share without interrupting others?"*

"Are there some ways you could make this task more interesting to yourself?"

Cautions & Hints

- **Private Please.** If possible, give I-messages in private.
- **Feedback, Not Emotion.** Effective I-Messages do not give vent to irritation; they tell the student about the irritation. In a calm, nonirritated voice, the teacher explains the impact of the student's behavior. By remaining calm while giving an I-Message, we avoid the possible escalation of emotion and make it more likely the student can listen to the feedback.
- **Positive I-Messages.** Be sure to communicate the positive impact students are having on you with positive I-messages.

"When you keep trying even when the problems are difficult for you, it makes me feel proud to be a teacher. I know you value what we do in class."

"When all of you give me your full attention as you are doing right now, I feel proud to be a teacher. I know you value learning and what I am teaching you."

Win-Win Discipline
Kagan Publishing • 800.933.2667 • www.KaganOnline.com

Chapter 10

Moment-of-Disruption Structures

Table the Matter

The teacher uses Table the Matter to acknowledge the need to meet and discuss, while allowing time for emotions to settle down and for student and teacher reflection before meeting. *"Let's give this a rest for now. We can talk about it later when we are both calm."*

Ideal Outcomes

- Class disruption is minimized.

- The meeting occurs after emotions have cooled down.

- The teacher has a chance to think of options.

- The teacher maintains a same-side orientation, even during a confrontation.

- The student feels his or her issues will be taken seriously.

- Table the Matter models a positive process students can internalize: not making decisions in the heat of a confrontation.

- The student learns self-control.

Recommended for...
Disruption: Aggression, Confrontation
Position: Angry, Control-Seeking
Individual or Class: Both

Moment-of-Disruption Structures

Table the Matter

1. Acknowledge the Student's Feelings

The teacher acknowledges the student's feelings, using a validating tone and/or phrase. *"You are really angry about this."*

"I understand you feel the grade was unfair."

2. Indicate Need to Reschedule

The teacher makes a firm, but friendly statement indicating that this is not an appropriate time to discuss the problem. *"This is not an appropriate time to discuss this…"*

"I can't stop the lesson to discuss this now…"

3. Suggest Appropriate Time

The teacher makes a statement about when an appropriate time might be to discuss the matter. *"…but, I will be happy to discuss this with you after the lesson."*

"Let's meet right after school to talk this over. I'm sure we can find a solution."

"Your concerns are important. I look forward to working out a solution with you."

4. Meet with the Student

In a follow-up, the teacher meets with the student to discuss and resolve the problem at a time that does not interrupt the learning process. Begin the follow-up by acknowledging how much better it is to talk after emotions have cooled down. Continue to validate the student's position, without necessarily accepting the student's point of view or request. *"I understand how hard you worked on the project and how disappointed you are that you received a poor grade after all that work. That must feel unfair. I wish I could give grades based on effort only. I really do appreciate your effort. But we have agreed to grade based on our rubric. Let's review the rubric we agreed on…"*

Chapter 10: Moment-of-Disruption Structures

Table the Matter *(continued)*

Cautions & Hints

- **Voice.** The teacher uses a short, firm, but friendly tone, letting the student know that instructional time is not the appropriate time to discuss problems.
- **Jot It Down.** The teacher indicates in writing his or her commitment to dealing with the issue.

"This is very important. I want to be sure we deal with this later. Let me jot down a note to myself now, so we don't forget."

- **To You… To Me.** Often the "To You… To Me" structure is useful in the follow-up, validating the student position, but communicating that other points of view are possible.
- **Self-Disclosure.** Let the student know you are using Table the Matter to control your own reaction.

"I'm upset right now, so we will table this matter until later. That way, we will make a much wiser decision."

Part IV

Follow-Ups

Following a disruption, our primary concern is our ultimate goal: Learned Responsibility. Has the student learned a more responsible way to meet the needs of his or her position? If so, there is no need to follow up. If not, we need to meet with the student to help the student learn more responsible ways to meet his or her needs. What we do in the follow-up meeting depends on the type of disruption, the position of the student, and the degree to which the student is on a path toward learned responsibility.

Part IV: Follow-Ups

In This Part

Chapter 11: Following Up 113

Chapter 12: Follow-Up Structures 121

Chapter 11

Following Up

Chapter 11

Following Up

There are many possible ways to follow up after a disruption. We can have meetings of different types with the disruptive students, with the class as a whole, with parents, administrators, counselors, or a school team. We can reexamine and/or change our curriculum, instruction, or management. We can use a range of follow-up structures. Or we could do nothing.

We respond differently depending on the type of disruption, the position of the student or students, and of course, their history of disruptive behavior. In this chapter, we overview the range of possible follow-ups and when to use each. But before presenting how to follow up, we will ask if we should follow up, and why we have follow-ups.

Pillar 1
Same-Side

Pillar 2
Collaborative Solutions

Pillar 3
Learned Responsibility

When to Follow Up

Often following a disruption, no follow-up is necessary. The student has responded to our moment-of-disruption intervention, senses we are on the same-side, and is learning more responsible behavior. A follow-up is necessary only if, following the disruption, we feel we are not making progress toward putting the Win-Win three pillars in place. Some form of follow-up is necessary if, following our response to a disruption, the disruptive student:

1. Does not experience us to be on the same-side.
2. Does not accept the discipline response.
3. Is not learning more responsible behaviors.

Following Up

Thus, to determine if a follow-up is necessary, we ask three questions related to the three pillars:

1. **Same-Side:** Does the student feel I understand where he or she is coming from, that I am on the student's side?
2. **Collaborative Solution:** Does the student accept the discipline solution, identify with it—feel it is a reasonable response to the disruption?
3. **Learned Responsibility:** Is the student learning to act responsibly; over time is the student becoming less disruptive?

If the student senses we are on the same-side, accepts and identifies with the discipline solution, and is learning to be more responsible, there is no need to follow up.

Why Follow Up?

Follow-ups are a second chance. Often in the heated moment of a disruption, it is not possible to do more than reorient the disruptive student and his or her classmates to the learning task. There is not enough time or calm to implement the three pillars. For example, a quick strategy to reorient a disengaged, bored student might be to use the student's name in a teaching example and/or to use proximity, walking over and standing close to the student while continuing a presentation.

Chapter 11

Following Up

While name dropping or proximity might work to solve the discipline problem in the moment, the teacher may not have communicated he or she is on the same-side as the student, the student did not participate in creating a discipline solution, and the student may not have learned more responsible behavior. In Win-Win Discipline, we do not reject discipline strategies which quickly reoriented students to learning without implementing the three pillars. We see those strategies, though, as only short-term, stopgap patches, not long-term cures. The follow-up is a chance to go beyond stopgap measures—a second chance to put the pillars in place.

The ultimate goal of Win-Win Discipline is Learned Responsibility. We want students leaving our classrooms to have learned responsible, nondisruptive ways to meet their needs. Positioning ourselves on the same-side with our students, validating their positions, cocreating discipline solutions, and helping students accept the need to learn responsible behaviors are all means to helping our students achieve learned responsibility.

Learned Responsibility Differs for Each Position

Because each position is associated with different needs, and disruptive behaviors are disruptive attempts to meet those needs, learned responsibility involves a different kind of learning for each position. We want students to fill their needs responsibly without teacher prompting. We want them to reach the level of autonomous responsibility.

Following Up

Reaching the level of autonomous responsibility involves a different kind of learning for each position. For example, the student who is in an Angry position needs to learn to recognize early warning signs and cool-down procedures that work for him or her. The student who is avoiding failure needs to learn how to seek help from teammates, classmates, teachers, and other adults. In each case, obtaining autonomous responsibility means learning important life skills.

How to Follow Up

Following a disruption, we have many options. At one end of the continuum, we may feel the disruption was handled well, the student is on the path toward acquiring a responsible orientation, and so there is no need to follow up. At the other end of the continuum, we may feel we have exhausted our own resources and the student is still showing no progress toward learned responsibility. In that case, we may turn to outside support such as an administrator, a school counselor, or a school support team. Usually, the situation falls somewhere between these two extremes.

The Four Approaches

There are four primary follow-up approaches:

1. **Preestablish new or reestablish old preventive procedures.**
2. **Establish moment-of-disruption procedures for the next disruption.**
3. **Implement follow-up structures.**
4. **Offer a life skill training.**

Chapter 11

Following Up

Establishing Preventive Procedures

Depending on the type of disruptive behavior and the position of the student, we may want to establish preventive procedures or reinforce existing preventive procedures. For example, if the disruption occurred due to disengagement, we would examine the many procedures to eliminate or minimize disengagement. If the disruption occurred because the student was seeking control, we would examine ways to give the student more autonomy like offering choices, giving students more responsibility, or changing our language from *"You need to…"* to *"The responsible thing to do is…"*

Establishing Moment-of-Disruption Procedures

Depending on the type of disruption, we may need to establish with the student exactly what will happen if that type of disruption occurs again. For example, following an angry outburst, we may establish with the student nonverbal cues to use if we see a build up of anger or frustration. The cue may signal that the student needs to visit the cool-down area or use one of the many other ways to cool down.

Following Up

Implementing Follow-Up Structures

There are six progressively controlling follow-up structures. The structures vary in intent. For example, establishing a Contract that spells out the consequences for the next disruption and makes future disruptions less likely because the consequences are not desirable for the student. In contrast, having a Same-Side Chat builds a positive student-teacher relationship and makes future disruptions less likely because students don't want to disrupt the class of a teacher who cares about them. Sample Follow-Up structures are detailed in the next chapter.

Life-Skill Training

The *Win-Win Discipline* book includes an extensive summary of the need for life-skill training, types of life skills, and approaches to life-skill training. The primary types of life skills:

1. Emotional Intelligence
2. Character Education
3. Habits of Success
4. Development of Multiple Intelligences

Two well-articulated life-skill programs:

1. The Prepare Curriculum
2. Skillstreaming

Chapter 11

Following Up

Life Skills Aligned to the Seven Positions

There are critical life skills which help students meet the needs associated with the seven positions. Win-Win Discipline reaches its ultimate goal of Learned Responsibility to the extent it promotes these seven life skills:

Life Skills for the Seven Positions

Position	Life Skill
Attention-Seeking	**Self-Validation:** Validate oneself instead of turning to external sources of positive attention.
Avoiding Failure	**Self-Confidence:** Seek help rather than avoid talk. Make attributions that lead to optimism rather than helplessness.
Angry	**Self-Control:** Spot the signs of mounting anger and learn cool-down techniques rather than acting out the anger.
Control-Seeking	**Self-Determination:** Define one's choices rather than trying to establish control by rejecting others.
Energetic	**Self-Directing:** Direct one's energy in productive ways.
Bored	**Self-Motivation:** Restructure tasks to convert boredom to engagement.
Socially Uninformed	**Self-Informing:** Inform oneself when uncertain about rules or procedures.

Chapter 12

Follow-Up Structures

Chapter 12
Follow-Up Structures

Win-Win offers six follow-up structures, differing in degree of control. This is symbolized by a Progressive Follow-Up Wheel.

Least controlling of the student is the Same-Side Chat. Here we don't tell students how to behave or even discuss disruptive behaviors. We form a positive relationship with the student by showing interest and caring. It seems almost paradoxical: without dealing with a student's disruptive behavior, via the Same-Side Chat, often we have a dramatic impact on reducing the student's disruptive behavior. Mid-level in degree of controlling the student is Replacement Behavior. Here the teacher works with the student to generate more responsible behavior, models the behavior, and guides the student in practicing the behavior. Far more controlling is a Parent Conference. The teacher meets with the parent(s) of the disruptive student, generating solutions and holding the parent(s) accountable for working with the teacher to implement solutions.

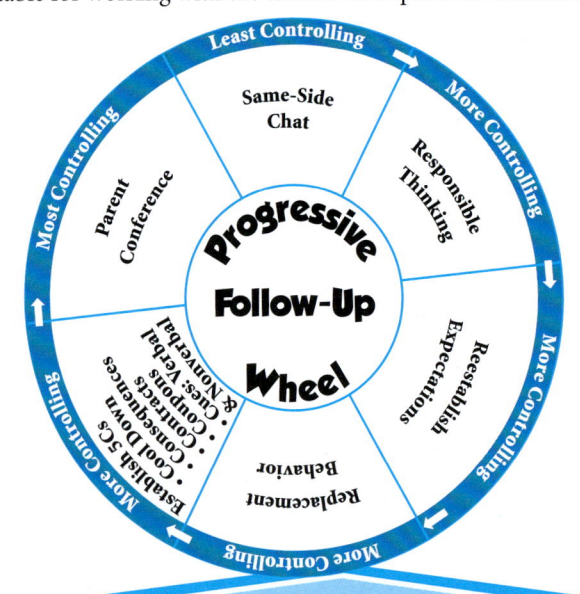

Progressive Follow-Up Wheel

- Least Controlling: **Same-Side Chat**
- More Controlling: **Responsible Thinking**
- More Controlling: **Reestablish Expectations**
- More Controlling: **Replacement Behavior**
- More Controlling: **Establish SC** — Cool Down, Contracts, Coupons, Cues: Verbal & Nonverbal
- Most Controlling: **Parent Conference**

Win-Win Discipline
Kagan Publishing • 800.933.2667 • www.KaganOnline.com

Follow-Up Structures

Here we give details of three sample Win-Win Follow-Up Structures:

- ◆ **Same-Side Chat**
- ◆ **Responsible Thinking**
- ◆ **Contracts**

In the book *Win-Win Discipline,* more Follow-Up Structures are provided. Each of the three selected structures has different functions:

Same-Side Chat allows us to better understand a student's position and better establish a same-side orientation. By communicating that we care about, are interested in, and are empathetic toward the student, we go a long way to eliminating future disruptions. Students don't want to disrupt the class of a teacher who cares about them.

Responsible Thinking Many students lack a moral compass. They don't direct their behavior based on moral principles. The Responsible Thinking follow-up structure helps students guide their behavior by asking three questions:

1. **Win-Win:** *"Have I considered the needs of others as well as my own?"*
2. **Respect Others:** *"Have I treated others the way I would like to be treated?"*
3. **What If Everyone:** *"What would happen if everyone behaved the way I did?"*

Contracts clarify an agreement by the student to act responsibly going forward. They clarify expectations, help students remember, identify with, and live up to their agreement to replace disruptive behavior with responsible behavior.

Chapter 12

Follow-Up Structures

Same-Side Chat

When we don't understand a student's position and/or don't feel ourselves to be on the same-side with the student, we schedule a meeting to get to know the student better and to develop empathy with him or her so we can honestly place ourselves on "the same-side" with the student.

Ideal Outcomes

- We better understand student position(s).

- We feel more empathetic toward the student—on the same-side.

- We establish rapport with the student.

- The student feels received and understood.

- The student is more open to share responsibility and to learn more responsible behaviors.

- Feeling more understood, that you are on his or her side, the student is less likely to be disruptive.

Recommended for...
Disruption: Confrontation
Position: Attention-Seeking, Control-Seeking
Individual or Class: Individual

Follow-Up Structures

Same-Side Chat

1. Schedule a Meeting
Set a time and place to meet so you and the student will not be interrupted. *"Johnny, I would like to get to know you better. Would you be willing to meet with me after class? I don't have any agenda other than to get to know you a little better."*

2. Meet
Indicate at the outset of the meeting that you have no other agenda than to get to know the student better. Let the student know you will not be talking about school. *"I would really like to know you a bit better. I would like to know what your life is like outside of school. Is that OK with you?"*

3. Stay in Student Comfort Zone
Do not probe. Let the student feel comfortable and talk about what he or she would like to share. Give the student choices as to what to talk about. *"Can you tell me a little bit about yourself, like some of the things you most like to do, or about your family or friends?"*

4. Positive Closure
After the meeting, let the student know you in fact have enjoyed getting to know him or her better, and invite future contact. *"I have enjoyed talking with you. I especially enjoyed learning that _____. If you would like to chat again sometime, please let me know and I will do the same. It helps me to get to know my students a bit better."*

Follow-Up Structures

Same-Side Chat *(continued)*

Cautions & Hints

- **Follow the Lead of the Student.** Discuss what he or she would like, giving the student choices as to topics. Do not focus on the student's disruptive classroom behaviors. Stay within his or her comfort zone. As the student is ready, explore family, friends, likes, dislikes, aspirations, and fears —but only as the student is ready.
- **Be Empathetic.** Maintain an empathetic, nonanalytic, nonjudgmental, nonmanipulative manner. Don't try to change the student or figure him or her out. Assume a relaxed, casual posture and language.
- **Don't Play Analyst.** Don't worry about determining the student position—that will emerge when the student trusts you.
- **Same-Side.** Attempt as much as possible to feel what it is like to be the student and let the student know you know you are putting yourself in his or her place: *"I can see how you would feel _____ (sad, angry, happy, fearful, embarrassed…). That would have made me really angry."*
- **Use Reflection.** Use reflective, noninterpretative language. OK: *"You really like it when you are chosen for the team."* Not OK: *"Being chosen for the team makes you feel included."*

Follow-Up Structures

Responsible Thinking

Students are guided toward responsible thinking via three questions: (1) Have they considered the needs of others as well as their own—sought a Win-Win solution? (2) Have they have treated others as they would hope to be treated? and (3) Have they have acted the way they would hope everyone would act?

Ideal Outcomes

- Students develop empathy and perspective-taking skills.

- Students develop impulse control and self-management skills.

- Students become more self-aware.

- Students learn to consider the impact of their behavior on others.

- Students learn to evaluate options by potential outcomes.

- Students learn to ask the 3W questions.

- Students become more responsible.

Recommended for...
Disruption: Breaking the Rules
Position: Angry
Individual or Class: Both

Chapter 12

Follow-Up Structures

Responsible Thinking (continued)

Steps

1. Express Desire to Give Student Skills

The teacher lets the student know that he or she wants to share a critical-thinking skill. *"Sam, I want to share with you a critical question that will help you make better decisions. The question will help you be successful in getting what you want and help you help others as well. Are you interested?"* [Note: Although there are three responsible thinking questions, each follow-up deals with only one.]

2. Obtain Buy-In

The teacher discusses advantages of responsible thinking until the student expresses interest. *"I find that in deciding what to do, there is a critical question to consider. If I take time to ask this question, I make better decisions for myself and for others. Would you like to learn about this question?"* [Stay at this step until student expresses desire to learn the question.]

3a. Question 1: Win-Win?

The teacher engages the student(s) with Responsible Thinking Question 1: *"What would be a Win-Win solution? What would meet the needs of everyone involved? Let's start with what we want. For example, let's say someone took my book. What do I want?* [Teacher works with student to list desired outcomes such as get the book back, have the person say he or she is sorry, be sure it won't happen again…]. *Once I am very clear on the desired outcomes, it is a lot easier to decide how to act. Will hitting the person get me what I want? Will taking his or her book do it? What will get me what I really want?*

"Now let's ask what the other person wants. Did he or she take your book because of wanting the book or because of anger toward you? If your classmate wants the book, is there a way you could share, or is there a way that classmate could get his or her own? If the person is angry at you, is there a way you could work through it to dispel the anger? Can we find a Win-Win solution—a way you both could get what you want or need?"

Follow-Up Structures

Responsible Thinking *(continued)*

Steps *(continued)*

3b. Question 2: Which Way Would I Like...?

The teacher engages the student(s) with Responsible Thinking Question 2: *"How would you like to be treated? Have you treated others that way? If we treat others the way we would like to be treated, usually we will feel good about ourselves, they will feel fairly treated, and we will maintain good relations."*

3c. Question 3: What Would Happen If Everyone...?

The teacher engages the student(s) with Responsible Thinking Question 3: *"What would happen if everyone acted that way? What would happen if everyone drove as fast as he or she wanted? What would happen if everyone just chose any side of the road to drive on? What if everyone hit others whenever they got angry? What kind of class would we have?"*

4. Practice

The teacher has the student(s) practice using the responsible thinking question that is the focus of the follow-up, applying the question to the student's own disruptive behavior. *"Let's try the responsible thinking question."* [The teacher has the student try applying the question first on some disruptive behavior the student has not done such as wandering around the room, not bringing in homework, hitting a classmate, carving on a desk, or making fun of a classmate. When the student shows the ability to apply the responsible thinking question to the behavior of others, the teacher has the student apply the question to his or her own disruptive behavior. If the student cannot apply the responsible thinking questions, the teacher then models applying it.]

5. Elicit Willingness

The teacher works with the student to elicit willingness to apply the question on an ongoing basis. *"Are you willing to try it? I'm sure that if you did, you would be an excellent model for others and improve relations in our class."*

Chapter 12

Follow-Up Structures

Responsible Thinking (continued)

Cautions & Hints

- **One Approach at a Time.** Work on only one of the responsible thinking questions at a time. Make sure the student is applying that approach before working on a second one.
- **Sidestep Resistance.** If the student is resistant to applying the responsible thinking question to his or her own behavior, start with historical, literary, or imaginary examples. Only later move on to self-evaluation.
- **Private Talk.** Work in private with students as you try to foster responsible thinking.
- **Same-Side.** Communicate to students that you know what they are feeling. *"I have had things taken before and it really gets me angry."*
- **Foster Empathy.** Work with the student so he or she can understand what it feels like to be someone who is yelled at or hit. *"Have you ever had someone yell at you and accuse you…?"*

Follow-Up Structures

Contracts

By creating a written contract, the teacher and student clarify the agreement and increase the probability that the student will remember, identify with, and live up to it.

Ideal Outcomes

- Student and teacher are very clear on their roles and their agreement.

- Commitment by the student is strengthened.

- Student and teacher have a document to refer to later to check on fulfillment.

- Students learn to keep commitments and follow through on agreements and plans.

Recommended for...
Disruption: Aggression, Confrontation
Position: Angry, Control-Seeking, Energetic
Individual or Class: Individual

Chapter 12

Follow-Up Structures

Contracts (continued)

Steps

1. Express Caring
The teacher demonstrates that he or she cares for the student and wants to support the student in choosing responsible behaviors. *"Anne, I care about you and want to help."*

2. Establish Need
The need for a contract is established. The teacher describes the specific disruptive behavior and "mirrors" the student's behavior. *"This is a serious concern. Let me show you what it looks like."*

3. Describe Problem in Writing
The teacher and the student give a written description of the specific problem. *"Let's start by describing the behaviors that are occurring that are causing disruptions to learning. Let's list together exactly what is going on at the time of disruptions. [List behaviors]. _____. Let's see if we can agree on what the problem is. [Discussion]. Do we agree that the problem is (written statement)?"*

4. Generate and Record Solution
The teacher and the student explore various solutions. The student and/or the teacher generate and record the agreement. *"What do you think are some solutions? Let's jot down our best ideas _____."*

"Once we agree on a solution—what we are both going to do to solve it—let's make an official agreement between the two of us, a contract!"

"So, which one of these do you think will work?"

"Now let's agree to and record a solution we both feel good about."

5. Create Incentive
The student and/or the teacher choose and record an incentive that will motivate the student to follow through on the plan. *"If you can do this, the payoff for you is _____."*

6. Establish Consequences
The teacher and the student select and record a logical consequence if the disruptive behavior is repeated. *"But we both agree that if you choose to continue to _____, then the consequence will be _____."*

Follow-Up Structures

Contracts (continued)

Steps (continued)

7. Commit to Contract, Establish Accountability

The teacher and the student solidify the contract agreements by signing the contract. Parent(s) also signs the contract, when appropriate. A time line is established for the contract and monitoring strategies. *"Now that we agree to this contract, let's both sign it and make it official. Let's decide when we will meet to review how it is going."*

8. Explore Position, Temptations, Commitment

When sufficient trust has been established, explore with the student his or her position. [What are the needs met by the disruptive behavior? What are the temptations to break the contract?] The teacher may share his or her perspective on the student's position, but the focus is on helping the student open up in a self-discovery process, not on telling the student.

Position

"It seems to me that you are pretty (angry, discouraged, bored). Am I off-base or pretty close?"

"No one likes to be told what to do. From what you are telling me, it sounds like homework assignments feel like that—being told what to do. Let's see if we can turn that around. One idea is to allow you some choice about what the assignment will be, or how you will present it…"

"We all like to be the center of attention sometimes. It is tempting to crack a joke. What could you tell yourself or do when you are tempted…?"

Temptations

"This contract means changing your behavior, and it is hard for all of us to break old habits. What part of the contract do you think will be difficult for you?"

"What might lead you to break the contract?"

Commitment

"In what ways are you going to remind yourself of our contract? What are you going to do to make sure you live up to it?"

"This may be difficult to stick to. What are you going to do when you are tempted to _____?"

Chapter 12

Follow-Up Structures

Contracts *(continued)*

Cautions & Hints

- **Pace.** Don't rush the process; contracts are mutual, not imposed.
- **Be Sincere.** Don't say you care about the student if it is not honest that day. Students will know.
- **Positive, Not Negative.** Emphasis is on alternative behaviors, not "stopping the disruptive behaviors." OK: Student agrees to keep hands to self. NOT OK: Student agrees not to touch other students. This point is very important. In the unconscious, the negative is lost; therefore, an agreement not to touch others calls up a mental picture of touching others, which becomes more likely. In contrast, an agreement to keep one's hands to oneself calls up the image of hands to oneself, which is more likely to be realized.

Negative agreements often actually increase the probability of the prohibited disruptive behavior.

- **Same-Side Mirror.** Let students know you are not mocking them—that you are trying to help them see themselves as others see them.
- **Validate Input.** Validate student input and suggestions.
- **Multiple Disruptive Behaviors.** If there are several disruptive behaviors, the contract focuses on one or two that are good starting points.
- **Student Language.** Use student language in writing up the contract.
- **Concrete Language.** Describe the problem as specific, concrete, objective behaviors, not effects of behaviors. OK: Johnny taps his pencil on his desk, plays with Susie's hair, and makes strange noises. NOT OK: Johnny annoys others.
- **Student Input.** Imposed incentives and consequences won't work. Shared responsibility is the key to a collaborative solution.
- **Explore Temptations.** When the contract is established and signed, explore what might lead the student not to fulfill the contract and how the student can avoid temptations.
- **Congratulate.** Use nonverbal and verbal praise when you see the student acting in accord with the contract. Take a moment to congratulate the student.

Part V

Conclusion

The foundation of Win-Win Discipline is empathy. Empathy gives us a new set of lenses: We focus on students' unmet needs rather than their disruptive behaviors. This focus creates a same-side orientation, so we create collaborative solutions and teach rather than discipline our students. We seek with our students win-win solutions, helping them learn ways to meet their needs without being disruptive.

Chapter 13: Conclusion

Win-Win Discipline is a transformative approach to classroom discipline based on a few simple premises. By assuming that disruptive behavior is motivated behavior, we look beyond behavior to see if there are non-disruptive ways students can meet their needs. As a result, we look at disruptive students with new eyes. Instead of a bad student needing to be disciplined, we see a student who has not learned responsible ways to meet his or her needs.

With this new set of lenses, we transform our approach to discipline. Instead of discipling our students, our goal is to teach them more responsible ways of behaving. Students win (they replace self-defeating behavior with skills they use for a lifetime), classmates win (they suffer less time stolen from learning, fewer embarrassments, and less bullying), and teachers win (they spend their time as teachers rather than as disciplinarians). After all, none of us got into the teaching profession to discipline students; we entered the profession to teach students skills to help them lead more successful lives.

Win-Win Discipline transforms discipline. We no longer discipline students. We help students acquire discipline. We direct our efforts in helping students learn responsible ways to meet their needs.

Part VI

Notes

As we practice the philosophy and techniques of Win-Win Discipline, we expand our skill set. We learn more successful ways to relate to our students. A helpful tool in this process is to take notes—to record what works best for us to prevent disruptive behavior, to respond to students in the moment-of-disruption, and to create winning follow-ups.

Prevention: ABCD Disruptions

A _____

B _____

C _____

D

Prevention: The Seven Positions

- Attention-Seeking
- Avoiding Failure
- Angry
- Control-Seeking

- Energetic
- Bored
- Socially Uninformed

Win-Win Discipline
Kagan Publishing • 800.933.2667 • www.KaganOnline.com

Moment-of-Disruption: ABCD

A

_____

B

_____

C

_____

D

Moment-of-Disruption: The Seven Positions

Attention-Seeking

Energetic

Avoiding Failure

Bored

Angry

Control-Seeking

Socially Uninformed

Win-Win Discipline
Kagan Publishing • 800.933.2667 • www.KaganOnline.com

Follow-Ups

Same-Side Chat

Responsible Thinking

Contracts

About the Author

Dr. Spencer Kagan is an internationally acclaimed researcher, presenter, and author of 20 books, and over 80 book chapters and scientific journal articles. He is a former clinical psychologist and full professor of psychology and education at the University of California. He has received honorary doctorates from two universities. Dr. Kagan is the principal author of the single most comprehensive book for educators in each of five fields: cooperative learning, brain-friendly teaching, multiple intelligences, classroom discipline, and classroom energizers. Dr. Kagan developed the structural approach to instruction. He has created many popular brain-based, cooperative learning, and multiple intelligences structures like Numbered Heads Together, Timed Pair Share, and Number Group Mania! Dr. Kagan is the founder and codirector of Kagan Publishing and Professional Development, a company dedicated to improving the lives of teachers and students. Dr. Kagan has provided workshops and keynotes in over 38 countries. Dr. Kagan's books are translated into many languages, and his instructional strategies are used in teacher training institutes in many countries.

Kagan

It's All About Engagement!

Kagan is the world leader in creating active engagement in the classroom. Experience the power of a Kagan Workshop.

Kagan Workshops:
- Cooperative Learning
- Win-Win Discipline
- Brain-Friendly Teaching
- Kagan Coaching
- Social-Emotional Learning (SEL)
- Subject-Specific Workshops
- Trainers and Administrators

Check out Kagan's line of books, SmartCards, software, electronics, and hands-on learning resources—all designed to boost engagement in your classroom.

Kagan Products:
- Books
- SmartCards
- Software
- Spinners
- Learning Chips
- Posters
- Learning Cubes

Win-Win Discipline
Kagan Publishing • 800.933.2667 • www.KaganOnline.com